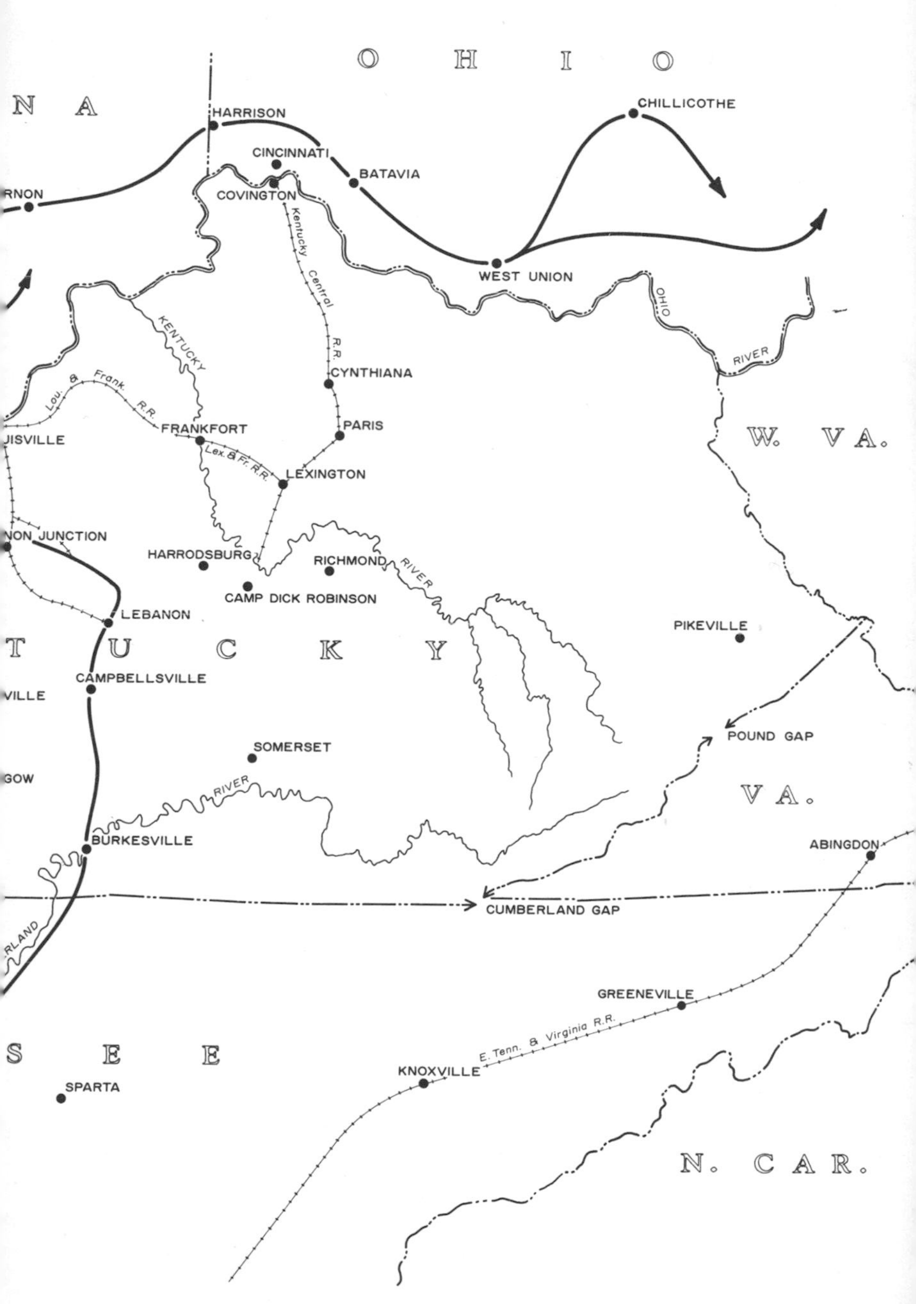
OHIO
NA
HARRISON
CHILLICOTHE
CINCINNATI
BATAVIA
RNON
COVINGTON
Kentucky Central R.R.
WEST UNION
OHIO
RIVER
KENTUCKY
Lou. & Frank. R.R.
CYNTHIANA
FRANKFORT
PARIS
JISVILLE
Lex. & Fr. R.R.
LEXINGTON
W. VA.
NON JUNCTION
HARRODSBURG
RICHMOND
RIVER
CAMP DICK ROBINSON
LEBANON
PIKEVILLE
TUCKY
CAMPBELLSVILLE
VILLE
POUND GAP
SOMERSET
GOW
RIVER
VA.
BURKESVILLE
ABINGDON
CUMBERLAND GAP
RLAND
GREENEVILLE
E. Tenn. & Virginia R.R.
SEE
KNOXVILLE
SPARTA
N. CAR.

The Kentucky Bicentennial Bookshelf
Sponsored by

KENTUCKY HISTORICAL EVENTS CELEBRATION COMMISSION
KENTUCKY FEDERATION OF WOMEN'S CLUBS

and Contributing Sponsors

AMERICAN FEDERAL SAVINGS & LOAN ASSOCIATION
ARMCO STEEL CORPORATION, ASHLAND WORKS
A. ARNOLD & SON TRANSFER & STORAGE CO., INC. / ASHLAND OIL, INC.
BEGLEY DRUG COMPANY / J. WINSTON COLEMAN, JR.
CONVENIENT INDUSTRIES OF AMERICA, INC.
In memory of MR. AND MRS. J. SHERMAN COOPER by their children
CORNING GLASS WORKS FOUNDATION / MRS. CLORA CORRELL
THE COURIER-JOURNAL AND THE LOUISVILLE TIMES
COVINGTON TRUST & BANKING COMPANY
MR. AND MRS. GEORGE P. CROUNSE / GEORGE E. EVANS, JR.
FARMERS BANK & CAPITAL TRUST COMPANY
FISHER-PRICE TOYS, MURRAY
MARY PAULINE FOX, M.D., in honor of Chloe Gifford
OSCAR HORNSBY INC. / OFFICE PRODUCTS DIVISION IBM CORPORATION
JERRY'S RESTAURANTS / ROBERT B. JEWELL
LEE S. JONES / KENTUCKIANA GIRL SCOUT COUNCIL
KENTUCKY BANKERS ASSOCIATION / KENTUCKY COAL ASSOCIATION, INC.
THE KENTUCKY JOCKEY CLUB, INC. / THE LEXINGTON WOMAN'S CLUB
LINCOLN INCOME LIFE INSURANCE COMPANY
LORILLARD A DIVISION OF LOEW'S THEATRES, INC.
LOUISVILLE & NASHVILLE RAILROAD
METROPOLITAN WOMAN'S CLUB OF LEXINGTON
BETTY HAGGIN MOLLOY
MUTUAL FEDERAL SAVINGS & LOAN ASSOCIATION
NATIONAL INDUSTRIES, INC. / RAND MCNALLY & COMPANY
PHILIP MORRIS, INCORPORATED / MRS. VICTOR SAMS
SHELL OIL COMPANY, LOUISVILLE
SOUTH CENTRAL BELL TELEPHONE COMPANY
SOUTHERN BELLE DAIRY CO. INC.
STANDARD OIL COMPANY (KENTUCKY)
STANDARD PRINTING CO., H. M. KESSLER, PRESIDENT
STATE BANK & TRUST COMPANY, RICHMOND
THOMAS INDUSTRIES INC. / TIP TOP COAL CO., INC.
MARY L. WISS, M.D. / YOUNGER WOMAN'S CLUB OF ST. MATTHEWS

John Hunt Morgan and His Raiders

EDISON H. THOMAS

THE UNIVERSITY PRESS OF KENTUCKY

Research for The Kentucky Bicentennial Bookshelf
is assisted by a grant from the
National Endowment for the Humanities.
Views expressed in the Bookshelf do not
necessarily represent those of the Endowment.

ISBN: 0-8131-0214-6

Library of Congress Catalog Card Number: 75-3553

A statewide cooperative scholarly publishing agency
serving Berea College, Centre College of Kentucky,
Eastern Kentucky University, Georgetown College,
Kentucky Historical Society, Kentucky State University,
Morehead State University, Murray State University,
Northern Kentucky State College, Transylvania University,
University of Kentucky, University of Louisville, and
Western Kentucky University.

Editorial and Sales Offices: Lexington, Kentucky 40506

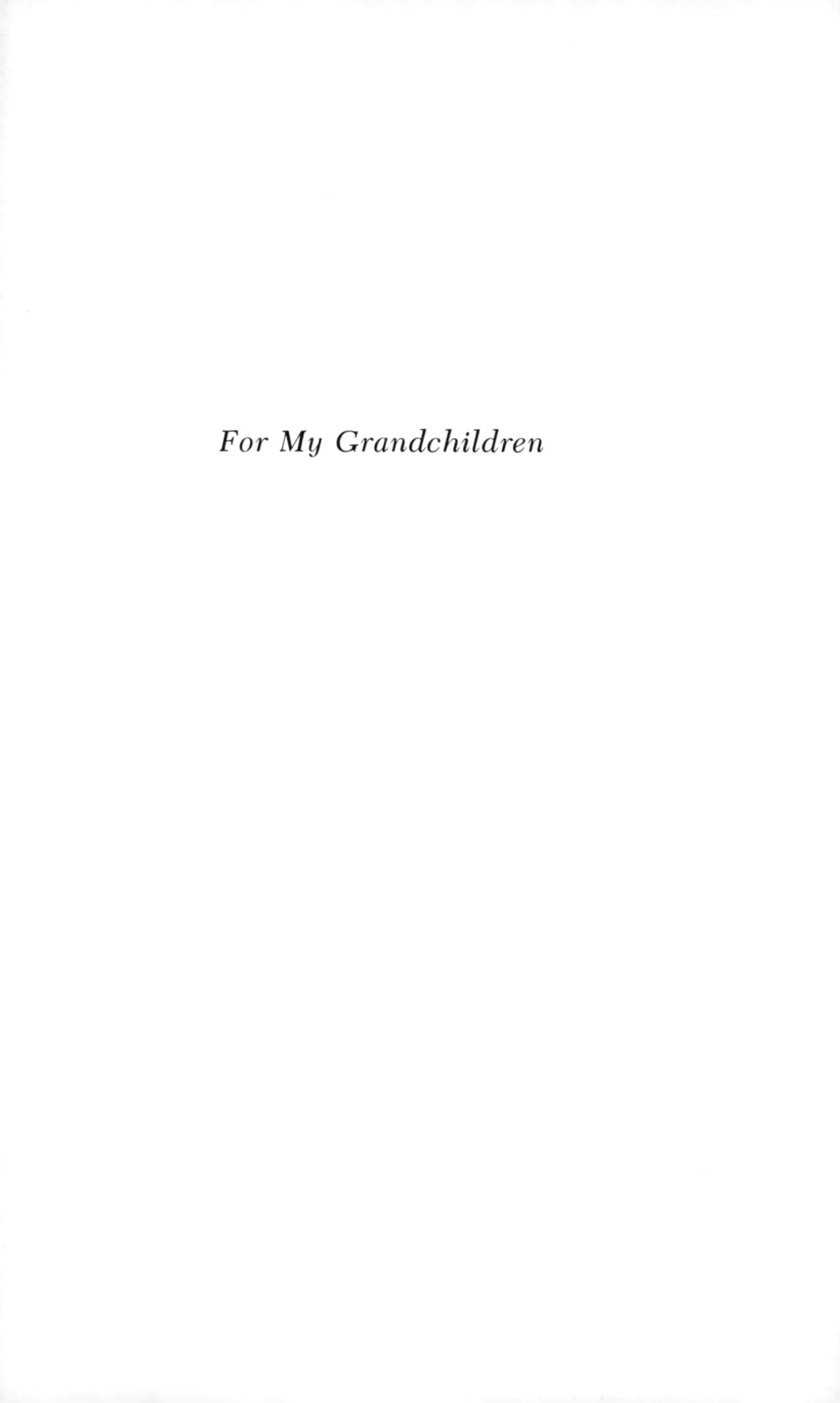

For My Grandchildren

Contents

Acknowledgments

THE WRITING of a manuscript of any length usually requires that the author seek help from various friends, acquaintances, and even strangers. This effort is no exception.

First, I am indebted to Woodson Knight, long-time colleague and friend, editor, and former journalist, who took time from his otherwise busy existence to read my final draft with a critical eye. Although he says that he is not an avid Morgan fan, he did admit that he is one of those many Kentuckians whose grandfather fought with the general.

Others contributing in different ways include: J. Winston Coleman, Jr., author and historian, Lexington, who furnished information on early-day Lexington and about General Morgan's death; Charles A. Hodgin, Kentucky Military Institute, Lyndon, who provided data about Morgan's military training at his institution; Mrs. R. D. Lawler, History Associates of Wilson County, Lebanon, Tennessee, who graciously supplied information concerning Johnnie Morgan Caldwell, the general's daughter; John Long, assistant to the executive editor, *Courier-Journal & Times*, Louisville, who arranged for the use of that publication's rare picture of the general and his mare, Black Bess; Jerry Mart, photographer, Hopkinsville, Kentucky, for the use of photo maps in the area of Ridgetop, Tennessee; Madie L. McIntosh, hostess, Hunt-Morgan Home, Lexington, for information about the Hunt and Morgan families; Robert Nash, Shiloh National Military Park, Shiloh, Tennessee, for maps of that battle area; Elmer G. Sulzer, author, historian, and former Indiana University professor, Sarasota, Florida, for invaluable reference data and other material; and James M. Terry, member of the L & N Railroad's legal staff, Louisville, for use of his original copy of Duke's history of the Raiders.

There are others, too, who provided encouragement and assistance, among them: the late Joe Creason, columnist for the *Louisville Courier-Journal;* Mrs. Harold Mullins, past president, Kentucky Federation of Women's Clubs, Valley Station; Mrs. Nettie Watson, library assistant, The Filson Club, Louisville; and my wife, Thelma, who provided helpful and critical comment while this manuscript was being written.

E.H.T.

Introduction

MANY SOUTHERNERS even today look upon John Hunt Morgan as a savior, a shining knight, or a Robin Hood. To the North during that troubled time, Morgan was sometimes a brigand and often a source of grief to the military command; Federal soldiers and civilians alike habitually referred to him as the Horse Thief. And in Kentucky, in particular, one is either for him or against him; there is no middle ground.

This daring soldier has become a bigger-than-life legend. He left no descendants, yet his name will live as long as Kentucky history continues to be written. Whatever his failings, John Morgan can take his place in history as a leader of men. He may not have always led them in the right direction, but he led them. He did his best work with a small group, usually not more than 600 men. Such groups could maneuver well, rush in, attack, and rush out, then gallop off across the countryside either to safety or to another strike, miles away.

Through Morgan's great personal magnetism he was able to round up some of Kentucky's finest and most daring young men. In time men from all parts of the state—more than 10,000 in all—served under his command. This often lends credence to the long familiar claim "My grandfather fought with Morgan." However, if all of those claims were truthful, Morgan might well have been able to change the outcome of the war.

In spite of his independence and his eagerness to branch out on his own, Morgan with but few exceptions worked within the framework of the overall strategy mapped out in conferences with his superior officers.

He had little time for paperwork, deplored routine, and hated humdrum camp life. Few of his superior officers understood his drive—least of all Braxton Bragg, who held a childish grudge forever because Morgan had been away in Kentucky when the Battle of Stone's River was fought.

Just why John Hunt Morgan did what he did has fascinated many researchers. Some say that it was the death of his first wife, Rebecca, which gave him the real will to take out his grief on the North. Whatever the drive, it seemed to find its direction after he had severed his ties with Lexington.

Many of the officers who served with him, including Basil W. Duke, believed that the general's enthusiasm for war became tempered after his second marriage. This can be refuted to a great extent, because some of his most daring raids were attempted after he had married Martha Ready in Tennessee. His direct disobedience of orders in crossing the Ohio came late in his career and must have given him much to think about during his capture and confinement. His daring escape from prison afterward is an adventure over which his followers still marvel.

By the time he made his last raid into Kentucky, Morgan was a tired and disillusioned man. Still attempting to be the bold cavalier, he may well have lost any real sense of the way the war was going. After all, things had changed since Shiloh, and although he may not have given it any consideration, the South had only a few great moments after that terrible battle. But as time passed, Morgan seemed to be obsessed with the desire to make "one more raid" into Kentucky. Unfortunately, this desire was not always shared by his men, many of whom during the latter part of his career, were no longer the elite of Kentucky manhood. Many men who took the places of the original members no longer felt pride in being Morgan's Raiders. Instead they became men to whom life did not mean a great deal. The bank robberies at Mount Sterling and Lexington were only two examples of just how insensitive the minds of his men had become. Such disregard for property had manifested itself even earlier—before the raid across the Ohio River—and certainly the wanton destruction and outright thievery demonstrated during the raid through Indiana and Ohio was an omen. By this time Morgan had completely lost control of discipline—he had never really had much—and he was a saddened and confused man as he returned to Virginia in defeat to live out his last few months.

The censure from his own men and the deeply resented Northern label, "King of the Horse Thieves," took its toll. The two men who admired him most, John Castleman and Basil Duke, commented on his change of appearance and outlook, his bitterness and despair, during those last days.

Morgan died as dramatically as he lived. It was only fitting that Duke inherit the lost cause. Patient and persistent, he was there to the end, as the president of the Confederacy was captured along with the last of Morgan's Raiders. One does not feel that Morgan would have taken a different path.

1

MORGAN THE MAN

DARKNESS CLOSED IN early that cool, crisp, autumn night. Only a few people were on the streets of Lexington, and most of those were on their way home to enjoy the warmth of families and firesides. Except for two hay wagons rumbling along the Versailles Pike, that dusty road was deserted.

By midnight the two wagons had reached Shryock's Ferry on the Kentucky River, seven miles west of Versailles. There they were met by twelve men on horseback, and soon, with calm precision, the men, horses, and wagons were transported across the river on the ferry. On the other side the group continued their journey. A glimmer of light had appeared in the east by the time they stopped at a remote farmhouse. A barn door opened silently, and the two wagons quickly disappeared inside with all but one of the riders.

The doors of the barn closed again, just as quickly, and the remaining rider turned his sleek, sweaty horse back in the direction of the ferry. John Hunt Morgan was returning to Lexington to complete the job he had begun.

Within a few hours, if all went well, he would have most of the other members of his Lexington Rifles convinced, and they, too, would be ready to join the Confederate army. With two wagonloads of guns from the

Lexington armory hidden under the hay and the small group in the barn, who already were snuggling down under their blankets to catch a few hours of sleep, Morgan's Raiders were on their way. It was September 21, 1861.

John Morgan gave the reins a quick flip and his steed obediently broke into a gallop. Both man and horse needed rest, but there was no time for that now. He thought of the guns and ammunition hidden deep in the hay of the two wagons—all that he and the members of the Lexington Rifles could get together at the armory and smuggle out of Lexington. There had been some tense moments, particularly when several Federal soldiers from Camp Dick Robinson had stopped by earlier in the evening, apparently to watch members of the Rifles practice their drills. But all had gone well. At the moment, he had 17 men. By nightfall, with luck and a bit of persuasion, he would have more; then he would need horses in abundance to put together a cavalry unit. That unit would be the best he could make it; he would settle for nothing less. He had made his decision, a pledge of honor to join and to defend—to death if that was what it took—what he believed in: the Confederate States of America.

There had been little doubt about where John Morgan's sympathies lay—a Confederate flag fluttered defiantly each day above his hemp mill in Lexington. Not all his fellow townsmen agreed with him. Some whom he had considered friends would cross the street to avoid him after his choice became known. Others openly pledged their support, for Lexington was a divided city in a divided state.

Morgan's devotion went farther back than the day he began flying the flag over his hemp mill—as far back, some said, as when he had organized the Lexington Rifles. At first it was considered a social organization, and Morgan was pleased that it contained on its roster the names of some of the most aristocratic families in all gave her husband their first-born. They named their little son John Hunt for Henrietta's father, who had come to Kentucky from his native Trenton, New Jersey, and bought a lot in the newly laid-out town of Lexington. The house he built there, Hopemont, was probably designed by Benjamin Latrobe. Later called Hunt-Morgan House, the old structure was to be preserved as a symbol of the gracious way of life so treasured by the Hunts and the Morgans.

In 1829 Calvin and Henrietta Morgan returned from Alabama to live in Lexington. Perhaps Henrietta was not satisfied to remain so far from her beloved Kentucky. Whatever the reason, the family returned to the Bluegrass and settled down on a farm that Henrietta's father owned on Tate's Creek Pike. There in the big, rambling brick house, Calvin and Henrietta raised eight children: six boys—John, Calvin, Richard, Charlton, Thomas, and Key—and two girls—Henrietta, who married Basil W. Duke, later to become second in command of Morgan's Raiders; and Kitty, who married Colonel Ambrose P. Hill.

John has been described as a very complex person, and undoubtedly he *was* the most complex of the family. At first appearance he was calm, easygoing, soft-spoken, and exceedingly courteous—a "typical" Southern gentleman, many said later. He had very little sense of discipline, and the lack of that quality would be one of his greatest weaknesses in the years of his life he was to spend in the service of the Confederacy. Those who knew him well said that he either lived the peak of the good life or, if things did not go as he had planned, plummeted to gloomy depths.

Life for young John certainly must have been lively on the Tate's Creek Pike farm with seven brothers and sisters, and—with moods such as his to be contended with—neither was life dull for others in the family. But aside from his enjoyment of the usual good life on a Bluegrass farm, little is known of John Morgan's early days. It must have been a busy time for him, as he shared whatever the family life called for, including rather extensive travel.

At the age of sixteen, John Morgan entered Transylvania College in Lexington. For that period of his life he moved into town to live with his grandfather, John Wesley Hunt, at Hopemont. The house stood on the corner of Second and Mill streets in Lexington opposite Gratz Park, and since Transylvania College was at the opposite end of the park, the young scholar had to walk only a short distance to attend classes.

John was described as a restless, undisciplined youth, and the first few weeks of school had scarcely passed before instructors and school administrators alike had concluded that he was not going to be an outstanding student. Perhaps it was attention he sought, and if that was his desire, he certainly achieved it. In time, after numerous escapades (though few were ever described in detail) Transylvania authorities became quite concerned. In one instance, John and a group of his classmates had congregated at the corner of Gratz Park and, according to one account, "used ungentlemanly language to passersby and strangers." Near the end of his second year at Transylvania he is said to have become involved in "a more serious difficulty" with another student. As a result, Morgan was suspended from school, and there is no record of any further formal education.

Four years later, in 1846, twenty-one-year-old John and his brother Calvin, along with Alexander Morgan, their uncle, left Kentucky to fight in the Mexican War. They joined the First Kentucky Cavalry at Louisville, and John was commissioned lieutenant, a circumstance that probably helped to fashion the young man's thinking for years to come.

Uncle Alex and his two nephews reached Mexico in time to participate in the Battle of Buena Vista. Two other prominent Kentucky-born men participated in that battle: one was the commanding officer of the U.S.

forces, General Zachary Taylor, later to become president of the United States; the other was a young lieutenant, Jefferson Davis, who married the general's daughter and was to become the president of the Confederate States of America.

Alexander Morgan was killed during that battle, and John and Calvin were mustered out July 8, 1847, at New Orleans. As they were on their way back to Lexington a few weeks later aboard a Mississippi River steamboat, John assured his brother that when he reached home he was going to settle down and go into business. As he explained it, he would not need any more excitement for quite a few years.

John Morgan entered business as he had planned, acquiring a hemp factory and a woolen mill. Both ventures prospered despite the dire warnings of many who had known John as an immature youth (including some officials at Transylvania).

Apparently his activities were not entirely confined to business. On November 21 of that same year John married Rebecca Gratz Bruce. Only eighteen years old, young Rebecca lived with her parents in the "Bradford House," on the corner just across Second Street from Hopemont. During John's short college career, he had seen her as a young girl with pigtails who stared at him as he raced in and out of Hopemont. When she grew to womanhood it was his turn to stare at her as their love blossomed.

Rebecca Bruce Morgan was an appealing woman with a childlike face. Rather quiet and somewhat frail, she was described as a "mild person imbued in no ordinary degree with the Christian graces of gentleness, meekness, forebearance and long suffering." After the wedding, she and John settled down in the home with her parents.

John Morgan's business continued to thrive and he branched out into buying and selling slaves. He also became active in community affairs. He had been accepted into the Masonic Lodge before he went to Mexico; now he became a captain in the Union Volunteer Fire Department, a member of the city council and the school board, and a communicant of Christ Church. He pledged generous contributions to his "alma mater," Transylvania College. John Hunt Morgan had matured considerably during the years since he had been expelled from the very college which he was now helping to support.

Tragedy touched John and Rebecca in 1853 when they lost their infant son—whether it was stillborn or died soon after birth is now not certain. Always delicate and frail, Rebecca became an invalid shortly afterwards, a fact that burdened John's mind.

Time passed, and Rebecca slowly withered, as one put it, "like a delicate spring flower." John became morose and frustrated because there seemed to be so little he could do to make her more comfortable. Perhaps this, if nothing more, contributed to his drive and determination to make something out of the Lexington Rifles, something more meaningful than their flashy green and gold uniforms.

Events that affected John Hunt Morgan, would occur in rather rapid succession in 1861. The Confederacy was formed in February; on April 12 Fort Sumter took a beating from Confederate gunfire, as Kentucky-born Major Robert J. Anderson, the commanding officer, felt the force of that first battle. Despite all this, Kentucky attempted to remain neutral; at least, the majority of Kentuckians neither favored secession from the Union nor felt they should yield to political pressure from the seceded states. Some opposed the idea of fence straddling—since the state opposed secession, it must be pro-Union. But Kentuckians were different; they always had been, ever since they had formed a state in 1792. They had no desire to see force used against the Southern states; nor did they desire that their state leave the

Union they had worked so hard to join. Kentucky had become the fifteenth state, and loyal sons wanted it to remain that way. Many newspapers throughout the commonwealth, including the Louisville dailies, advocated neutrality. George Prentice, editor of the *Louisville Daily Journal,* denounced the suggestion that Kentucky secede as "a wild, unpatriotic, and insane idea." Later, as the war progressed, two of Prentice's sons served and died with the Confederate army. Even then he was never able to write anything good about the Confederacy.

Kentucky remained a divided state in many areas, but it became largely pro-Union. This probably had no bearing on John Morgan's decision. Apparently his mind had been made up, perhaps as far back as the days long before Fort Sumter when he was drilling with the Lexington Rifles. Yes, he would join the Confederate army. If that should not prove possible, he would move out on his own, take the Lexington Rifles with him into the field as an independent outfit, and help out where needed.

The Confederate flag continued to fly defiantly in the breeze from the sturdy pole atop his hemp mill on Georgetown Street. Now that he had decided definitely and irrevocably to take his chances with the Confederacy, he had a lot of work to do. The summer of 1861 would be a busy one for Morgan. It would be a short war, he was sure of that, and helping to keep it short would be outfits such as the one he planned to form from the Rifles. They would make quick work of any armies the Federals could mount.

It was in April of that year that President Lincoln issued a call for volunteers, and that month a message was received by the governor of Kentucky:

Washington, April 15, 1861

To His Excellency, Hon. Beriah Magoffin, Governor of Kentucky:

Call is made on you by tonight's mail for four regiments of militia for immediate service.

Simon Cameron, Secretary of War.

The governor fired back this reply the same day:

Frankfort, April 15, 1861.

Hon. Simon Cameron, Secretary of War, Washington City:

Your dispatch is reviewed. In answer, I say, *emphatically*, Kentucky will furnish no troops for the wicked purpose of subduing her sister Southern states.

Yours, B. Magoffin, Governor of Ky.

However Kentuckians felt about the governor's reply, many families throughout the commonwealth lived in an uneasy suspension of time as news of the grim and ugly possibilities of war began to creep into their daily lives. Many would make their choice, and in Kentucky, as in no other state, these painful decisions would divide communities and families, in some instances for years after the war ended.

A speech by John J. Crittenden on April 17, 1861, did not increase John Morgan's peace of mind. Speaking before an overflow crowd at Lexington, Crittenden, a Kentucky representative in Congress, urged that the state take no part in a war that would pit brother against brother. Instead, he said, Kentucky should stand firm in the attitude of a peacemaker and warn both sides against involving the nation in a civil war with the terrible consequences that were sure to follow.

"Let us not be forced into civil strife for the North, nor dragged into it for the South—take no part with either." Kentucky had done nothing to bring the war about, he said, and he pointed out that "she had not invited it, it was against her interest, she should do nothing to promote it; but by all moral force of her position, she should bravely hold on to the flag of the Union, and under its broad folds extend the hand of conciliation to both."

John Morgan left the hall after Crittenden's speech not as a man in a dilemma but as one who knew what he wanted to do. In his mind there was no place in Kentucky for a peacemaker, not until the day when the Union should be brought to the realization that Southerners, too, had hearts, emotions, and beliefs.

In the background of political speeches, continued rumors of war, and persistent attempts at neutrality, a lively social life went on in Lexington. John's sister Henrietta married Basil W. Duke on June 18, 1861. The wedding was held (as sister Kitty's would be, two weeks later) in the large parlor adjacent to the front hall at Hopemont. The affair was one of the most important events of the Lexington summer social season, and every woman there admired Henrietta's choice. Basil Duke had gone to Saint Louis to practice law after his graduation from Transylvania. He later returned to Lexington and by 1861 was a member of the Kentucky legislature. After the fall of Fort Sumter, the twenty-three-year-old's first move was to volunteer his services to help protect Kentucky either in its stand for neutrality or as a state in the Confederacy.

No one knows for sure just when he decided to join his brother-in-law in his plans for the Lexington Rifles. Certainly at the time of the wedding, Basil Duke had not dreamed he was destined to follow Morgan to fame.

Neither he nor John Morgan gave much thought to the fact that their carefree way of life would soon be gone, probably forever. Days for horsetrading, cock fights, and shooting matches would be over, and the gracious, often luxurious, way of life in Fayette County would disappear. Even such staples as country-cured hams and Kentucky bourbon would eventually be hard to come by.

In July 1861, less than a month after Henrietta Morgan became Mrs. Basil Duke, Rebecca Bruce Morgan, the "delicate spring flower" of John Morgan's life, died. With his beloved Rebecca gone, nothing remained to prevent him from giving the Confederacy everything he had—even himself.

Though his despondency knew no limits, Morgan rallied and, with a resolution that only he could conjure, proceeded with his plans to join the Confederate army.

2

A SWEARING IN

In August 1861 a short item appeared in the *Lexington Observer and Reporter:* "Some excitement has risen among our citizens in reference to an encampment of recruits for the United States Army, said to be organized in the county of Garrard. . . ."

Thus was noted the establishment of a military camp on the Dick Robinson farm near the Dix River, scarcely more than twenty-five miles south of Lexington. The very presence of such a camp in the Bluegrass so near the city infuriated many Confederate sympathizers, including John Hunt Morgan.

"We have been assured by some of the principal officers of the encampment that there is no intention on their part, or on the part of the government to use these men for aggressive purposes," the item continued. "The reason given for the establishment of this camp is the defense of our state from an apprehended invasion of Kentucky by Tennessee."

The pro-Union editor of the newspaper, Daniel Carmichael Wickliffe, added that in his opinion the fears of Union aggression were entirely groundless and that the troops should be removed as soon as the supposed necessity of their presence disappeared.

Actually, the camp had been established by a group of Union sympathizers headed by Garrett Davis of Bourbon County, a former Whig congressman, and William

Nelson, native of Maysville and a graduate of the U.S. Naval Academy. Nelson recently had transferred to the army as a brigadier general. Stationed at Washington, D.C., he was sent to Kentucky, some say at his own request, and placed in charge at Camp Robinson.

Deeply concerned that Kentucky's neutrality was being openly violated by the establishment of Camp Robinson, Governor Magoffin sent commissioners to President Lincoln in Washington to urge the removal of this force from within the limits of his commonwealth.

Lincoln, with a bit of Kentucky logic—after all, he too was a native of the Bluegrass State—said that the soldiers at the new camp consisted exclusively of Kentuckians in the vicinity of their own homes, and that the force had been raised at the urgent solicitation of many of their friends and neighbors. With that statement, the president declined to order the camp removed.

In the meantime, another shipment of guns from the North, consigned to General Nelson at Camp Robinson, arrived at Lexington over the Kentucky Central Railroad. The report was circulated that John Morgan and members of the Lexington Rifles planned to seize them.

After a warning by a trusted informer in Lexington, General Nelson dispatched a regiment of cavalry to the city to protect his precious "Lincoln guns," as they had been named by Confederate sympathizers.

A crowd had gathered on Lexington's Main Street, and as the Federal troops rode past the Phoenix Hotel, a civilian heckler yelled an offensive remark. One of the soldiers stopped his horse, pointed his rifle toward the crowd, and almost started a panic. Several women screamed, alarming a lookout for the Lexington Rifles stationed on the roof of the armory at the corner of Main and Upper streets nearby. He promptly blew a bugle call—a signal for members of the Rifles to assemble at the armory. Seconds later, the bell in the court house tower alerted the pro-Union Home Guards.

With a battle shaping up on Lexington's Main Street,

John C. Breckinridge, a United States Senator and Confederate sympathizer, hurried to the armory, where, after some discussion, he persuaded Morgan to call off his Rifles. "This is not the proper time," he is said to have told him, but he added: "Wait, your opportunity will come."

The Federal regiment with the "Lincoln guns" in tow, rode off toward Camp Robinson. Members of the Rifles and the Home Guard dispersed, and a sullen truce marked the passing of another crisis.

Events that would close the gates on Kentucky's hope for a peaceful coexistence with both North and South began to occur in rapid succession. First, Tennessee, which had also leaned toward neutrality, capitulated and was admitted to the Confederate states on July 22, 1861. President Jefferson Davis placed his West Point classmate Leonidas Polk, now an Episcopal bishop, in charge of its military operations.

The Confederacy also established a general line of defense against the North and placed Kentucky-born Albert Sidney Johnston, Polk's roommate at West Point, in charge of military operations in all of Tennessee, Arkansas, Kentucky, and a portion of Missouri. The defense line ran from Columbus, Kentucky, on the Mississippi River, east by way of Fort Henry on the Tennessee River and Fort Donelson on the Cumberland (both in Tennessee), northeast through Bowling Green, Kentucky, across Kentucky to Mill Springs on the Upper Cumberland River, southeast to Cumberland Gap, and extending into Virginia. This was a long, exceedingly thin line, one which even the Confederates must have had doubts about being able to defend with any marked success.

Under Major General Polk's command, 11,000 Confederate troops from Tennessee moved into Kentucky on September 3, 1861, and fortified strong positions at Hickman and Columbus on the western end of the defense line.

On September 5, Federal troops under Brigadier General Ulysses S. Grant at Cairo, Illinois, moved up the Ohio River and occupied two strategic points in Kentucky: Paducah, at the confluence of the Tennessee and the Ohio, and Smithland, some twelve miles farther upriver at the mouth of the Cumberland. Both the Tennessee and the Cumberland ran perpendicular to the Confederate line here and later would serve Grant as natural highways.

As the full impact of these various political and military maneuvers began to be understood, thoughts of war sobered those who loved Kentucky. They were coming to realize that, piece by piece, their curtain of neutrality was being torn away.

At Frankfort, Governor Magoffin, whose administration was said to contain a number of Southern sympathizers, tried to maintain his policy of keeping Kentucky neutral. The General Assembly had convened September 2, the day before General Polk occupied Hickman and Columbus, and—Southern sympathizers notwithstanding—again affirmed that the state would remain neutral. The next day a special committee was appointed to ask General Polk to withdraw from Kentucky immediately, but only a few short hours after the news of Polk's action, word reached Frankfort that Confederate General Felix K. Zollicoffer had moved three regiments into southeastern Kentucky in the vicinity of Cumberland Gap "to defend the other end of the Confederate line."

At that point the legislature ordered the U.S. flag flown from the staff above the capitol at Frankfort. With this gesture the attitude of Kentucky's General Assembly toward the Union was made clear. The Confederacy had violated the state's expressed desire for neutrality, and as a result of this action the Southern cause was lost in the Bluegrass State.

For all practical purposes, actual hostilities began in Kentucky the day General Polk made his move. After

General Grant had occupied Paducah and Smithland, General Johnston ordered General Simon Bolivar Buckner, with 5,000 Confederate troops then encamped just south of the Tennessee state line, to occupy Bowling Green. On September 18, Buckner proceeded to that strategic point on the railroad supply line. An advance detail was dispatched north of Bowling Green as far as the Rolling Fork River only thirty-one miles south of Louisville, where, in one spectacular move, they burned the railroad trestle across that stream. When the news reached Louisville it almost caused a panic. Most authorities, civil and military, believed that Buckner, who had been in command of the Kentucky State Guard before the war, planned an immediate attack on the city.

Brigadier General Robert J. Anderson had moved his headquarters to his native city of Louisville after the fall of Fort Sumter. In the face of Buckner's assumed threat, he ordered General William T. Sherman, then in command of the Federal troops at Louisville, to set up headquarters at Lebanon Junction with as large a force as he could muster, including members of the Louisville Home Guard. Here he would be in position to block any move to attack the city.

Two days later, with the threat of actual war and bloodshed hanging heavy over Kentucky, and with John C. Breckinridge's encouragement still ringing in his ears, John Hunt Morgan left Lexington with his force of 17 men and two wagonloads of guns to join General Buckner's command at Bowling Green.

When Morgan reached Green River on September 30, some 200 men had attached themselves to his unofficial command. Actually, it was a rather motley looking group by the time it reached the Confederate camp near Woodsonville in Hart County. For Morgan, however, the arrival was something of a homecoming. His uncle, Colonel Thomas Hunt, was there in command of two companies, and so was Morgan's old friend, Colonel Roger Hanson. A homely little figure with a rather peculiar stance, Colonel Hanson did not look much like a military man; nevertheless, he had the complete respect of his 600-man infantry regiment. Morgan and Hanson had served together during the Mexican War, and at Woodsonville in the days that followed they set out to shape their groups into some semblance of a military organization. Hampered by short supply of nearly everything, even that early in the war, Morgan was particularly frustrated in his attempt to organize a cavalry unit without a sufficient number of horses. A shortage of good horses would be a familiar problem for Morgan as the war progressed, and in this instance, the cavalrymen who had no steeds to mount were pressed into service in the infantry.

October continued cool and clear, and Morgan and Hanson took advantage of the good weather to concentrate on their daily drills. Morgan's brother-in-law, Basil Duke, had joined them early that month, and he assisted with the training, instructing the men in the intricacies of military life and in the use of firearms. For those who had horses, there were drills and turns to master, although they were to learn through bitter experience that these were very often useless when it came to actual combat on horseback. In time they would improvise their own often rather unorthodox cavalry maneuvers to fit the individual situation.

During the war many officers, especially those who had attended West Point, made much of Morgan's lack of formal military training. Historians today tend to minimize his experience as an officer in the Mexican War, and few realize that he studied military tactics at Kentucky Military Institute, an experience that probably accounts for his avid interest in the organization of the Lexington Rifles. Officials of the now defunct military school, later moved from its original location near Frankfort to Lyndon, Kentucky, say that Morgan and his brother Thomas attended in 1858 in connection with the training of the Kentucky State Guard, organized that year by General Buckner under appointment by the governor. As it turned out, Buckner, Morgan, and all the other cadets at K.M.I. later became officers—seven of them generals—in either the Confederate or the Federal army.

Now Morgan was doing his work well at Woodsonville. In a few short weeks, 84 well-trained men were mounted, fully equipped and ready to serve the Confederacy. The Green River Baptist Church at Woodsonville had been serving as headquarters, and it was in front of that building, later burned by the Federals, that Morgan and his men lined up one day in the warm, bright October sunshine to be sworn into the Confederate army. Coming up from headquarters specifically to do the honors was Major William P. Johnston, son of the commanding general.

Immediately after the swearing-in ceremony, the group elected officers. As might have been expected, Morgan was named captain; Basil Duke was his first lieutenant; James West, second lieutenant, and Van Buren Sellers, third lieutenant. Thus officially ended Morgan's first love, the Lexington Rifles, and in its place had been formed the nucleus of what eventually would be the Second Kentucky Cavalry.

Alike in their sense of purpose, Morgan and Duke could hardly have been more different in personal appearance. Morgan stood an even six feet tall and weighed about 185 pounds. "His personal appearance and carriage were striking and graceful," one description stated, ". . . his features were eminently handsome and he usually wore a pleasing expression. His eyes were small, of a grayish blue color, and their glances keen and thoughtful. . . . His constitution seemed impervious to the effects of privation and exposure, and it was scarcely possible to perceive that he suffered from fatigue or lack of sleep."

Duke, a native of the Georgetown area, was of slight build and weighed scarcely 130 pounds. He had angular features, dark hair, and dark penetrating eyes. Probably his most identifiable feature was his massive, jutting jaw. Although Duke has more than once been called the brains of the raid, there was nothing overbearing about him, and many said he was a very steadying influence on the more flamboyant Morgan. He attended Georgetown and Centre colleges before studying law at Transylvania.

On November 4, 1861, a special order from General Johnston, who had moved his headquarters from Nashville, Tennessee, to Bowling Green, was delivered to the Woodsonville encampment: "Captain J. H. Morgan's company will proceed without delay to Bowling Green and report for duty."

Although the autumn foliage was somewhat past its prime, bright splashes of yellow, red, and russet were still visible on that rather chilly November morning as John Hunt Morgan and his company departed the Woodsonville camp for Bowling Green. There were other things on the minds of the men, however, besides the array of fall colors. In the first place, Morgan's command had grown. In addition to his own men, three other cavalry units in training at the same time at Woodsonville had asked to join his ranks. Morgan welcomed them, and now, as they rode along the dusty Louisville-Bowling Green turnpike, they displayed an unaccustomed seriousness and quietness, as each man seemed to be alone with his personal thoughts. Up to now, for Morgan's men the war had not been a reality. They had participated in a few skirmishes during the assigned patrols, but to the men, those brushes with the enemy seemed little more than extensions of the fancy drills they had demonstrated as members of the Lexington Rifles at Crab Orchard Springs and the other summer resorts in the Bluegrass. It was true that two of the Raiders had been injured, but that first blood seemed only to whet their enthusiasm; the two injured men proudly wore their bandages as marks of courage and honor.

Now, as the command rode down the turnpike toward Bowling Green, stirring up clouds of dust, Morgan mused that for him things had not moved fast enough. He had left Lexington September 21, and now, seven weeks later, he still had not been involved in any really important action that would help win the war. His thought was to get the war over with quickly, head back to Lexington, and run his mill or do the dozens of other things he enjoyed. Those who knew him well said John Morgan was a sentimental and compassionate man, not the kind who would revel in battle. According to Basil Duke, who probably knew him better than any other man who ever associated with him, Morgan had an "exceeding gentleness of disposition and unbounded generosity [and] his kindness and goodness of heart were proverbial."

At about one o'clock Morgan called for a rest stop, and his men made the use of it that would grow more familiar as the war went on. Near the roadside where the troops had dismounted were several persimmon trees, each heavily laden with pinkish fruit. As their horses munched tender, late-growing grass, many of the men industriously filled their hats and other containers with the tasty wild fruit and proceeded to fill their stomachs as well. Others picked black walnuts from under the trees on the opposite side of the road and soon were cracking them with stones and removing the kernels with their pocket knives. But as the men rested there beside the Louisville turnpike, basking in the warmth of a pale November sun, the reality of war did indeed seem a long way off.

Morgan's cavalry had scarcely settled down at Bowling Green before vanguards of the Federal army under the command of General Don Carlos Buell at Louisville began to move down the railroad, threatening the former camp at Woodsonville. It was only fitting that Morgan and his men make plans for their first real strike since they had become members of the Confederate army. Their orders were to let the Federals know that General Johnston would stand for no nonsense. How they were to do it would be up to Morgan.

Selecting scarcely more than 100 of his best-trained men and some of the finest horses in his command, Captain Morgan left camp early on a cold December day and headed north. His objective was the Louisville & Nashville Railroad bridge across Bacon's Creek near Bonnieville, sixty-five miles south of Louisville.

It wasn't much of a task to burn the trestle. The structure was made of wood piling about thirty feet high with stone masonry abutments at each end. When they arrived, a detail quickly gathered dry driftwood from the creek area, piled it high at the south end of the trestle, and set it on fire. Flames leaped quickly up the dry piling, and soon the crossties of the bridge floor also were burning briskly. More driftwood was added. Then, in a maneuver not described in military manuals, the entire detachment sat down on the creek bank, relaxed as if around a campfire, and watched until most of the trestle had burned to the ground. Later, with only embers left glowing in the darkness, Morgan ordered his men to regroup and head back south.

In the months to come, Morgan's cavalry would never earn any ribbons or any other awards for discipline, mainly because it had known so little from the beginning. This night's work was no exception and the men joked and laughed as they galloped back down the Louisville turnpike toward Bowling Green.

The burning of the Bacon's Creek bridge was a minor incident as far as the overall war effort was concerned. Probably no one except the railroad officials would have given much attention to it except for two things: it was the first of many strikes Morgan would make on the

L & N Railroad; and, in addition, it caused Morgan to receive his first notice in the national press. There was much good-natured banter in the camp a few weeks later when someone brought in a copy of *Frank Leslie's Illustrated Newspaper.* In it was a woodcut showing the burned out bridge at Bacon's Creek with a lone Federal horseman surveying the damage. With that issue, Americans both north and south had read their first news item about John Hunt Morgan. During the next three years there would be many more reports in the press.

After the Bacon's Creek incident, Morgan and his cavalry settled down for the winter at Bell's Tavern (known today as Park City), twenty-five miles east of Bowling Green. The settlement had originally been called Three Forks, since three important pioneer roads converged there.

Three Forks became known as Bell's Tavern because of an inn built by William Bell, a Revolutionary War veteran who settled there in 1820. Mr. Bell kept enlarging his original inn, adding wings to provide more accommodations until the rambling structure covered an exceptionally large area beside the turnpike. When the Civil War began, the rather ramshackled tavern was owned by Mrs. Robert Slaughter Bell, daughter-in-law of William Bell, and her two sons.

It was in the area around Bell's Tavern, not far from the railroad track, that the Confederates made camp. While Morgan, Duke, and other officers of the command occupied quarters in the tavern, the men pitched their tents near the unfinished stone walls of what was to be Mrs. Bell's new tavern. Buell's army, too, holed up in camps not far to the north, and there was little to do except ride endless patrols as each side made sure that the other was not up to anything.

The winter was as bleak as the autumn had been beautiful. By early January the penetrating cold was made more disagreeable by rain, which, in Kentucky's quick-changing weather, occasionally turned to sleet. It was indeed a dreary time, and boredom coupled with the discomforts of the cold had many of the former members of the Lexington Rifles thinking longingly of the solid comforts of their own firesides back in the Bluegrass.

3

THE BITTER TASTE OF BATTLE

In mid-February of 1862, Morgan and his command were camped at LaVergne, Tennessee, sixteen miles southeast of Nashville. Much had happened since those frigid, bone-chilling days in January back at Bell's Tavern.

First, the eastern end of the Confederate front had collapsed when General George H. Thomas and his Federal army clashed with General Felix K. Zollicoffer's men, who were encamped behind a mile-wide circle of breastworks on the Cumberland River near Mill Springs. The battle took place January 19 at nearby Logan's Crossroads. General Zollicoffer was killed here, and the Southerners fell back to Tennessee.

Second, General Grant had left Paducah and marched on Fort Henry, located just south of the state line on the Tennessee River. The small Confederate force there surrendered on February 6. Six days later, an agonizing battle began at Fort Donelson, twelve miles east on the Cumberland River. After four days of fighting, part of the time in bitter cold and driving snow, this fort also capitulated. Fleeing the night before, rather than face capture, was Morgan's Tennessee counterpart, Nathan Bedford Forrest, who forded backwater from the flooded Cumberland and led his cavalry unit to freedom in the surrounding hills. Generals John B. Floyd and Gideon Pillow escaped by steamboat that same night, leaving General Buckner saddled with the unhappy duty of negotiating surrender terms with Grant.

"Unconditional and immediate surrender," the Ohio-born general said in a note to Buckner the next day, and that was what he got.

Two days before the surrender of Fort Donelson, General Johnston, fearing that he would be trapped behind Federal lines at Bowling Green, prepared to march to Nashville. No one dared call it a retreat, not that early in the war, and certainly not John Hunt Morgan, whose cavalry rushed ahead of the army and crossed the bridge at Nashville two days later.

Upon arrival in the Tennessee capital Morgan was appalled at what he saw. Civilians were raiding supply boats on the Cumberland River, and warehouses full of military stores were being wantonly looted. The rabble soon grew in number and eventually got completely out of hand. Morgan joined forces with Forrest, who had arrived from Fort Donelson, to help restore order. They saved several thousand pounds of bacon and many other provisions, but much of the remainder had been carried off or thrown into the river.

Six days later Morgan and Forrest acted as rear guard for Johnston's army as it abandoned Nashville and marched toward Murfreesboro. As they left the city they looked back and saw the vanguard of General Buell's Army of the Ohio moving in. From that moment to war's end, Nashville was lost to the Confederacy.

Morgan was camped at LaVergne, between the two cities, but Johnston settled down in Murfreesboro, thirty-two miles southeast of Nashville. Strategically located on the Nashville & Chattanooga Railroad, the Confederate army was only one hundred twenty miles from Chattanooga on a rail line that reached all the way to Atlanta. Thus, supplies would be no problem. The general proceeded to reorganize his 11,000-man army, and Morgan and his Raiders were assigned to the command of John C. Breckinridge, Morgan's old friend who had helped to prevent a clash with Federals back in Lexington the summer before.

Always a man of action, Morgan conceived the idea of a night raid on Nashville from his camp at LaVergne. After discussing plans with General Breckinridge and General Johnston, he chose 15 men and headed for the nearby city. Darkness was closing in fast as they reached the outskirts of town, and no one paid any attention to these riders on horseback. Almost everyone on that cold, February twilight was already at home, huddled around the warmth of a fireplace.

It required a bit of exploring, but Morgan finally found his target—the steamboat *Minnetonka*—tied up at the Nashville wharf. After a brief consultation, he and his men decided to set the steamboat afire, cut it loose, and let it drift downstream toward some Federal gunboats tied up a short distance below. With luck, the gunboats might catch fire too. The job turned out to be more difficult than they had anticipated, mainly because the steamer was secured by chains instead of ropes. They set fire to the boat, but before they could finish their mission, their lookout signaled that Federals were approaching on horseback.

The Raiders quickly reassembled and fled. Unfortunately they did not flee fast enough, and one member—Peter Atherton—was killed. He was the first of many Raiders to meet this fate as the war lengthened.

On the last day of February 1862, Morgan was at Murfreesboro, standing in a cold drizzle of rain as he watched Johnston's army march away. There was something electrifying about that moment, despite the weather, and Morgan wanted to be a part of it. Now that the army was on the move he would surely get his chance. Johnston was heading for Corinth, Mississippi, and within five weeks these 11,000 men would be locked in the bloody struggle that has been recorded in history as the Battle of Shiloh.

Morgan would remember that February day with greater pleasure for another reason. General William J. Hardee asked Morgan to accompany him to the home of Colonel Charles Ready at Murfreesboro for a meeting about proposed cavalry movements. On this occasion Colonel Ready introduced Morgan to both of his daughters, Martha and Alice, but it was twenty-one-year-old Martha who caught the captain's eye. Although Mattie, as her friends called her, was fifteen years younger than Morgan, she was probably the real reason that he soon moved his base of military operations from LaVergne to Murfreesboro. Such transfers of operations sometimes had social as well as military significance, and John Morgan was not the kind of a man to pass up either one.

Morgan was now in command of three companies, and they spent most of their time patrolling the roads and trails of Middle Tennessee. With the intimate knowledge of the countryside thus gained, the men felt an ease of spirit and a comfort they had not experienced since those rather carefree days they spent encamped on the Green River at Woodsonville. The approach of spring helped, too. Each day brought a new warmth, and by mid-March, the wooded areas around Murfreesboro were beginning to brighten with blossoms of dogwood and redbud. With each glimpse of greening woodlands, the men seemed the more eager to get things moving so they could be on their way back to Kentucky.

Patrols notwithstanding, Morgan found plenty of time to visit the Ready home, where the genial Colonel Ready usually invited the equally genial captain to stay for dinner. Frequently, after the evening meal had been completed, they would retire to the parlor, and Mattie would sing a song or two while Morgan and her father had coffee. Sometimes there would be patrols of their own—just the two, Morgan and Mattie—riding horseback together over the winding country roads, past hundreds of cedars and through meadows brightening with the green of tender new grass. Not as attractive as Kentucky bluegrass, Morgan would tease Miss Ready, but with things being what they were, the war and all, he could forgive that deficiency in an otherwise peaceful setting.

The leisurely rides in the country continued as the romance blossomed, but this idyllic period was a brief one. On March 15, 1862, Morgan took time out to cut the Federal supply line—the railroad from Louisville. His target was a relief train headed from Bowling Green to a point south of Gallatin, Tennessee, to help get a derailed locomotive back on the track.

At Gallatin, in a fashion that would become one of Morgan's trademarks, the captain and his men stopped the train and put the locomotive out of operation. They then set fire to thirteen freight cars standing on a siding near the depot, burned the water house, and destroyed the machinery used for sawing wood and pumping water. When they had completed the job, the area around the Gallatin depot was in shambles. They rode away then, but it was a historic occasion of sorts—the Raiders had just completed their first major strike against the L & N Railroad.

Morgan returned to Murfreesboro, but his romance with Mattie Ready had to wait once more. Just four days after his Gallatin strike he received orders to join General Johnston's army in northern Mississippi. The Raiders departed immediately. Reporting to Johnston at Burnsville, near Corinth, on April 4, Morgan learned that he had been promoted to the rank of full colonel. He also learned that a huge battle in which he and his cavalry would participate was less than forty-eight hours away. This time there would be no railroad tracks to wreck, no bridges to burn, no darkness of night under which they could hide. This battle would be waged in the woods and underbrush, the marshes, and the few open fields near a little log church called Shiloh. There

Yankees and Confederates would clash with fierce and deadly intent. General Johnston and his Army of the Mississippi would be leading the offensive. Present to bolster his plan of attack were General Polk, who had come down from Columbus with his army and heavy guns intact; General Pierre Gustave Toutant Beauregard, on hand with several thousand men from Louisiana; General Braxton Bragg, who had arrived from Pensacola with 10,000 men; and the commands of Generals Hardee and Breckinridge. As planned by Johnston, the attack would be a complete surprise to General Grant and his Federals encamped along the banks of the Tennessee River near Pittsburg Landing.

Two days after Morgan and his men arrived, early on the balmy and clearing Sunday morning of April 6, 1862, with the rising sun adding warmth to newly opened blossoms in a nearby peach orchard, Albert Sidney Johnston inspired his army with the assurance that "the eyes of eight million people are resting upon you at this very moment." Farther along the line, a Confederate captain was instructing his men to "aim low."

Morgan's squadron was assigned to the First Kentucky Brigade under command of another Kentucky native, Colonel Robert P. Trabue. When the war began, Trabue was living in Mississippi, but he obtained permission to go to Kentucky and organize an outfit for the defense of the Confederacy. His brigade had been ordered to be ready for battle at daylight, and they moved into position just behind Polk's Corps, some four miles southwest of Shiloh church. During the five hours they waited, the Battle of Shiloh roared on its terrible way. Sounds of 80,000 muskets and nearly 200 guns of heavier caliber added an unrealness to the pastoral setting, as shot and shell whined across the three-mile-long battle line that had been hastily drawn between Owl and Lick creeks on the west side of the Tennessee River.

By the time the Raiders began to move toward the carnage that was taking place before their eyes,

Morgan's men realized that things were considerably different from anything they had ever encountered before. Basil Duke said later: "We listened to the hideous noise and thought how much larger the affair was than the skirmishes on Green River."

As the battle continued, Morgan was separated from Colonel Trabue's First Kentucky. Eventually he began receiving his orders from General Hardee, whom he had accidentally encountered as they rushed about the field of battle. In the ensuing melee, the Raiders quickly learned that a wooded area was no place for a cavalry unit, and many of them dismounted and fought as infantry—a tactic they later would use to their advantage many times.

General Johnston had planned his attack well, but the vicious hand-to-hand combat took its toll; men fell—many wounded, many killed. Among them were Kentuckians fighting on each side. A pond on the battlefield would turn red with blood, and the action became so furious at a point along a sunken road that it would be known thereafter as the Hornet's Nest.

The Raiders had expected nothing like this. Never had they imagined that war could be so cruel, so heartless, so immoral and indecent; and they wondered how there could be so sudden a death for so many. The harshness and the agony of the cries of dying young men—many of them still in their teens—rose above the awful sounds of combat, and such thoughts they may have had of fancy drills in the bright green and gold uniforms of the Lexington Rifles at Crab Orchard Springs quickly faded in the grimness of reality.

Among the officers of Morgan's original command back at Woodsonville when he was elected captain of the company, two were hit by Minié balls. James West was killed instantly, but Basil Duke, wounded in the shoulder, would live to fight again. Also injured was Morgan's brother Charlton, who was serving as an aide to Colonel Trabue.

Just as victory was in sight for the Confederates, there came a loss that may well have changed the course of the war. A stray bullet struck General Johnston in the right leg, slightly below the knee. Unaware of the injury, he rode to the rear of the line, pointing laughingly at one of his boots where another bullet had cut the sole in two without wounding his foot. At that moment Johnston swayed and almost fell from his saddle. Governor Harris of Tennessee caught him, and several men helped the general to the ground. Only then did they make the terrible discovery. The bullet in the leg had severed an artery; the general was bleeding to death. He died at approximately 2:30 that afternoon, but the battle continued.

Although Johnston did not live to know it, when darkness closed in that Sunday night and the fighting stopped, his army had won the day—and certainly this seemed one of the great moments of the Confederacy.

Later that night rain began to fall, gently at first, then in torrents as some would tell later; but the inclement weather failed to thwart General Buell, with his 25,000 men under forced march from Nashville or General Lew Wallace, with 5,000 more. Throughout the night they worked to transfer the two armies across the Tennessee River so they could be ready to join the battle when daylight came.

General Beauregard, who had replaced Johnston, was in charge of the Confederate army as Grant moved his Federals into place early Monday, April 7. The fighting began anew, as savage and as brutal as it had been the day before. Soon the 30,000 fresh troops began to make their presence felt, and the Confederates began to give ground in the direction of Corinth. With every yard lost went the fruits of victory over which Johnston had rejoiced only twenty-four hours before. Morgan's squadron and most of the regiments of the First Kentucky served as rear guard as the entire Confederate army abandoned the field and headed for Corinth.

Both sides claimed victory, but statistics may well indicate that nobody won. In those two days of struggle, 109,784 men had fought hand to hand in a bloody tangle, the effects of which would be felt in thousands of homes in many states both north and south for years to come. For when the grim totals were announced, 23,746 men were either dead, wounded or missing. Confederate losses were 10,699: 1,728 dead, 8,012 wounded, 959 missing. The Federals lost 13,047: 1,754 killed, 8,408 wounded, and 2,885 missing. Included in these figures were more than a thousand Kentuckians killed, wounded, and missing—680 Confederates and 500 Federals. Someone later said that the South never smiled again after Shiloh.

By April 23, with dark memories of that battle still vivid in his mind Colonel Morgan was beginning to prepare a 325-man outfit for additional raids in Tennessee and Kentucky. Members of the squadron busied themselves nailing new shoes on their horses, removing the grime of battle from themselves and their equipment, oiling and polishing their guns. In another area of the camp, cooks prepared rations for traveling. Later, the men would augment these rather monotonous rations with wild berries in season. In all likelihood, too, many of the men would shoot wild game along the way, and at night roast their kill over campfires. Pack mules were laden with extra ammunition, and Morgan, more pleased than he had been since he left Lexington, had tucked snugly away in his saddlebags a $15,000 war chest supplied by Beauregard to finance the expedition.

Within three days the Raiders were marching eastward. By sundown they had reached the Tennessee River where they stopped for the night. As the quietness of that April evening settled over their camp, not a single man, from Morgan to the lowest private, expressed any regrets at leaving Shiloh behind.

4

THE FIRST KENTUCKY RAID

EN ROUTE FROM Mississippi northeast across Tennessee, wherever Morgan stopped he and the Raiders received a warm welcome. At Pulaski hundreds of people turned out when word spread that Morgan's Raiders were in town. Admirers crowded around, many of them hoping only to touch Morgan's little mare, Black Bess. When the colonel stopped at the hitching post in front of the hotel, the crowd closed in just to stroke her coat. Others attempted to clip souvenir swatches of hair from her mane and tail.

Marching on, the Raiders crossed Stone's River and felt as if they were almost back home. Darkness was beginning to fall that rainy, wet evening of May 4 when they arrived at the outskirts of Lebanon, Tennessee, where they were again welcomed with open arms. The first round of drinks was on the house at every saloon in town, and soon all were crowded. Many people opened their homes and invited Morgan and his men to share their accommodations and food. The Tennessee and Kentucky welcome—"Help yourself, such as it is," meant in all modesty that the hosts had provided the best they had in store. What few pickets had been assigned duty just outside town soon became drenched while walking their posts in the rain, and nearby farmhouses were opened so they could come inside. The friendly farmers and their families also provided food and, on occasion, bottles with contents that helped to make the soldiers warm inside as well.

The celebrating continued well past midnight, and few besides the drenched pickets gave much thought to the fact that they were far inside enemy territory and only thirty miles east of Federally held Nashville. No orders were left for early rising the following morning. Thus, Morgan's defenses were down when Federal troops some 600 strong—one report said 2,000—rushed into Lebanon soon after dawn. But one alert guard, who lost his life in the process, was able to spread the alarm in time to enable the colonel and many of his men to mount their horses and head for safety. The chase by the Federals developed into what many of the Raiders later described with embarrassment as the "Lebanon Races," because so many of them had to gallop for miles on horseback in order to elude the pursuers.

It was not an orderly chase, to be sure, as Morgan and probably a hundred of his men roared off down the road toward Rome and Carthage. When the chase was over, Morgan, with only about a dozen of his men, wound up on the north bank of the Cumberland River opposite the little village of Rome, some twelve miles east of Lebanon. In their haste to escape across the river before the Federals arrived, they left their horses on the south bank because the ferry boat was not large enough to transport them all. Morgan had reluctantly left Black Bess too. A gift from Warren Viley of Stonewall, Woodford County, Kentucky, and sired by Drennan from a famous line of Bluegrass saddle stock, the little mare had been Morgan's faithful steed for many a weary mile. Now, as Morgan looked back, he could see her galloping aimlessly around, neighing plaintively, in an apparent attempt to find her master. The colonel also could see dozens of blue-clad Federals as they fanned out along the shore looking for stragglers. The Federals he would view many more times before the war was over, but it was the last time he would ever see Black Bess.

When the score was counted, Morgan had lost 108 men—65 captured, 17 killed, and 26 wounded. Federals listed 79 killed and 64 wounded.

Morgan's spirits hit bottom after the "Lebanon Races," but he quickly snapped back to his usual enthusiastic self because there was work to do. Trusting in their unique talent for existing off the land when the going became difficult, he and the small group on the north bank of the Cumberland set out to acquire more horses. On May 6, despite some entanglement with Federal patrols, the bedraggled little group reached Sparta, high in the mountains of Tennessee more than eighty miles east of Nashville. There, within a few days Morgan's spirits rose even higher when about 50 of his men who had escaped the "Races" straggled in from Lebanon. Included among the 50 were many of those who had been with Morgan since those early days at Woodsonville.

With the group now grown to a rather respectable size and with much of their old zest restored, what could be more appropriate than another raid into Kentucky? For the Raiders who were sons of the Bluegrass, it would be good to see those rolling, tree-covered hills and grassy fields again!

The decision was not a difficult one to make, and within a very short time, the Raiders were heading for Kentucky. There was a lot of the old familiar joking and singing as they rode along, and within two days, now a revitalized and rested group, Morgan and his Raiders were back in Green River country. Kentucky had never looked so good. Birds chirped merrily in trees fresh and green as only the softness of spring could make them, and the thought of another May in the Bluegrass State made it easy to forget the fact that they were now far into Federal territory. As a party of only 50 or 60 men, they would not have much of a chance if they were surrounded by Federals; but, Morgan reasoned, they had been surrounded before and managed to escape. If the occasion demanded, they could do it again.

Early on the morning of May 12, the saddle-weary men arrived at Cave City, a point on the railroad almost eighty-five miles south of Louisville. They moved quietly into the center of the little village where a freight train was standing north of the station. Methodically they set fire to the string of cars and fired a charge of powder under the engine, demolishing it. Shortly after the fire of the burning freight cars had died down, a southbound train rolled into town, its crew and passengers oblivious of the fact that Morgan was there. After an exchange of a few shots, which caused no damage, the train was captured. Most of the cars were filled with Federal soldiers, and the officer in charge, Major W. A. Coffey, was an old acquaintance of Morgan. Among the passengers were wives of several of the officers, one of whom pleaded tearfully with Morgan not to kill her husband. The colonel, always gallant and gracious in the presence of women, assured her that he had no intention of killing anyone and that her husband was no longer his prisoner, but hers. He decided not to burn the train, mainly because he did not want to deprive the women passengers of a place to rest while they were waiting to be rescued. He did search the train and, according to some reports, found a strongbox in one of the baggage cars which contained about $8,000 in Federal funds. After confiscating the money, Morgan invited Major Coffey and the ladies to join him and his Raiders for lunch at the hotel across the tracks. Then he paid the proprietor with part of the Federal money, placed Major Coffey aboard the train with a freshly written parole in his hand, and ordered the engineer to take everyone back to Louisville.

As the locomotive, in reverse, rounded the bend north of the Cave City depot, Morgan's group began to saddle up for their ride back across Kentucky. Within a few days they had reached Chattanooga, where General Bragg was assembling a brand new Army of the Tennessee.

Whatever the disgrace that might have been attached to the debacle at Lebanon, Morgan survived it. The raid on Cave City, planned not only to bolster his spirits but to help his reputation as well, seemed to have worked. Within three weeks Morgan was forming a new regiment of the Second Kentucky Cavalry. Among his new recruits were John B. Castleman, who had come to Chattanooga overland from Lexington, Kentucky, with 41 young men he had recruited for the express purpose of joining Morgan. Others joined the Second Kentucky at that time, many of whom would make names for themselves: Gordon E. Niles, who later would put together the first issue of a short-lived, but lively little newspaper known as the *Vidette;* Robert A. Alston, who would become Morgan's adjutant; Thomas H. Hines, close friend of Castleman, who would in time undertake much of Morgan's undercover work; George Ellsworth, who for some reason known only to himself, had come down from his native Canada to ride with Morgan and contribute his talents as a telegrapher; and George St. Leger Grenfell, an Englishman who carried letters of introduction from General Robert E. Lee and General Beauregard. The only explanation he ever made as to why he was involved in the American Civil War was, "If England is not at war, I go elsewhere to find one." From Mississippi, where he had been hospitalized since Shiloh, came Basil Duke, Morgan's dependable standby, with several men he had rounded up from the old command. Also with Duke was a group of Texans under Captain R. M. Gano, and the entire force had ridden their horses all the way across Tennessee to join the outfit. The capable and dependable Duke was reinstated in his old position as second in command, and promoted to the rank of lieutenant colonel.

By early June 1862 the future looked bright for the Second Kentucky. Morgan had been ordered to Knoxville where his men were undergoing a rigorous training with the army of General Kirby Smith, and there they were armed with a special kind of gun—the regular Enfield rifle with the barrel sawed off. It became the favorite weapon of the Raiders, and they used it more than any other throughout the remainder of the war. Duke and Grenfell had seen to it that training was intense. There would be no more stalling and fumbling around behind the infantry. From then on, the Raiders might or might not operate as a cavalry, depending on conditions; their maneuvers might or might not be the orthodox ones described in the textbooks, but the techniques they perfected would work exceedingly well for them.

Equipped with the newest in guns and uniforms, Morgan and his Second Kentucky marched out of Knoxville on July 4, 1862, bound for Sparta, Tennessee. Ahead of his command of 876 officers and men was a force of 60 scouts. Their trail led over the old Walton Road that had been laid out across that part of Tennessee in 1799. At Sparta, Morgan's columns headed north toward Celina, a little village on the Cumberland River, where, with luck, they could ford the stream and within a few miles be in Kentucky. Morgan's First Kentucky Raid was under way.

A pause at Celina in the heat of the July sunshine gave members of the Second Kentucky their last chance to check up on the needs of their horses. After all, the horse and saddle would be "home" for the next few weeks. The men knew they were going many miles into enemy territory. Just how far depended upon the plans—and sometimes the whims—of their leader, but wherever he led them they would go, especially now that they were heading back to Kentucky.

The command's first brush with Federals was at Tompkinsville, Kentucky, eighteen miles northwest of Celina. There, after a rather lively but short encounter, they overpowered the Federals, taking about 300 prisoners. The prisoners were no asset, but the Raiders were elated over the capture of a number of good horses and a generous supply of food, including scarce coffee and sugar. After assigning a detail to take the prisoners back to Tennessee to be paroled, Colonel Morgan headed for Glasgow. That stop was at the urging of a number of the men of the command whose families lived there, and their arrival signaled a gala evening in the Barren County seat. Some of those now reunited had received no word from one another since Shiloh.

Though sweet, the reunion at Glasgow was a short one. Morgan set out the next morning with only one purpose in mind, to leave his mark on Federally controlled Kentucky. Near Horse Cave, on the railroad thirty-three miles northeast of Bowling Green, a thunderstorm struck, and the men took shelter as best they could. Meanwhile, Ellsworth cut his personal telegraph key into the line connecting Louisville and Nashville. There, as lightning flashed and thunder rolled, he set to work trying to glean information about the location of enemy troops. Despite the electrical storm that at one point caused sparks to fly from his telegraph key (and gave him his nickname "Lightning"), he gathered enough information to enable Morgan to plan his march and elude efforts to capture him during the remainder of the stay in Kentucky.

With a file of information about the Federal forces in his saddlebags, Morgan headed northeast for Lebanon, marching by night through the increasingly hilly terrain. After a few hours of rest the columns of the Second Kentucky reached the Rolling Fork River six miles from Lebanon on the afternoon of July 11.

Suddenly bullets fired by Federals guarding the river crossing whizzed around the heads of those in the advance columns, but Basil Duke, who put a great deal of faith in a couple of guns the men affectionately called "bull pups," wheeled them into position. These guns could lob a shell accurately a distance of up to 800 yards, and after they had "barked" a few times, the Federals fled toward Lebanon. Before the evening was over, Morgan had taken the town without loss and had captured almost 200 soldiers guarding the Federal storehouses beside the railroad track. Men of the Second Kentucky set to work the next day destroying such items as sugar, coffee, flour, and a large supply of guns. The powder, cartridges, and caps were thrown into a nearby creek. The remainder, including a large stock of clothing, was burned. In all, according to figures released by the Federals, the damage amounted to $100,000. To make matters worse for the enemy, a number of recruits joined Morgan's command while it was at Lebanon.

The Second Kentucky left Marion County and after marching throughout the night via Springfield, entered Harrodsburg about nine o'clock the next morning. Harrodsburg was a stronghold of friends and relatives of the Raiders, and the welcome they received was sufficient to make those of Morgan's men who were not Kentuckians wish they were. A hasty but bountiful picnic was prepared and during the celebrating, Morgan managed to do a good deal of recruiting for his cause.

Morgan realized that he was now only twenty-eight miles from Lexington, where he and many of his men would dearly love to stop for a visit. In an attempt to accomplish this safely, he sent one detachment north of Lexington, to burn bridges on the Kentucky Central Railroad, and another group west, to damage the Lexington & Frankfort Railroad in the direction of Louisville. With both lines cut, he would have a good chance of making it to Lexington before Federals could interfere.

As the railroad bridges were being burned and track torn up, General Jeremiah Boyle, in command of the Federal troops at Louisville, was in a state of frenzy; so were the people of that city and of Cincinnati. Boyle began to fire off telegrams to Washington. One read: "MORGAN HAS OVER 1,500 MEN." Another said: "MORGAN IS DEVASTATING WITH FIRE AND SWORD." Finally President Lincoln wired General Halleck in Mississippi to look into the "stampede in Kentucky."

Morgan, still in Harrodsburg, was oblivious to the fact that this exchange of telegrams was going on. Ellsworth had been enjoying Kentucky hospitality, and the nearest telegraph line was at Danville, so he had had no opportunity to intercept any messages. Even as Morgan's columns marched out of town just before sunset, they still had hopes of stopping at Lexington. By daylight they had reached Shryock's Ferry on the Kentucky River, where members of the Lexington Rifles the previous September had crossed with the hay wagons loaded with guns.

The ferry had been sunk and Mr. Shryock was nowhere to be seen, but the Raiders bailed out the water and everyone was transferred across. They continued their march to Versailles, just twelve miles from Lexington. There they learned that the hoped-for visit to the heart of the Bluegrass was out of the question. Confederate sympathizers in Versailles told them the disappointing news that several thousand Federal troops were stationed in Lexington and dozens of camps were scattered around the outlying parts, particularly at all roads leading into town. Wisely, Morgan canceled his proposed triumphant march into the city and headed for Georgetown, where many of his men had friends and relatives. But he vowed that some day he would parade his men into Lexington.

It was at Georgetown that Gordon Niles found a print shop and set up and printed a recruiting poster. It was headed, "KENTUCKIANS!" and began, "I come to liber-

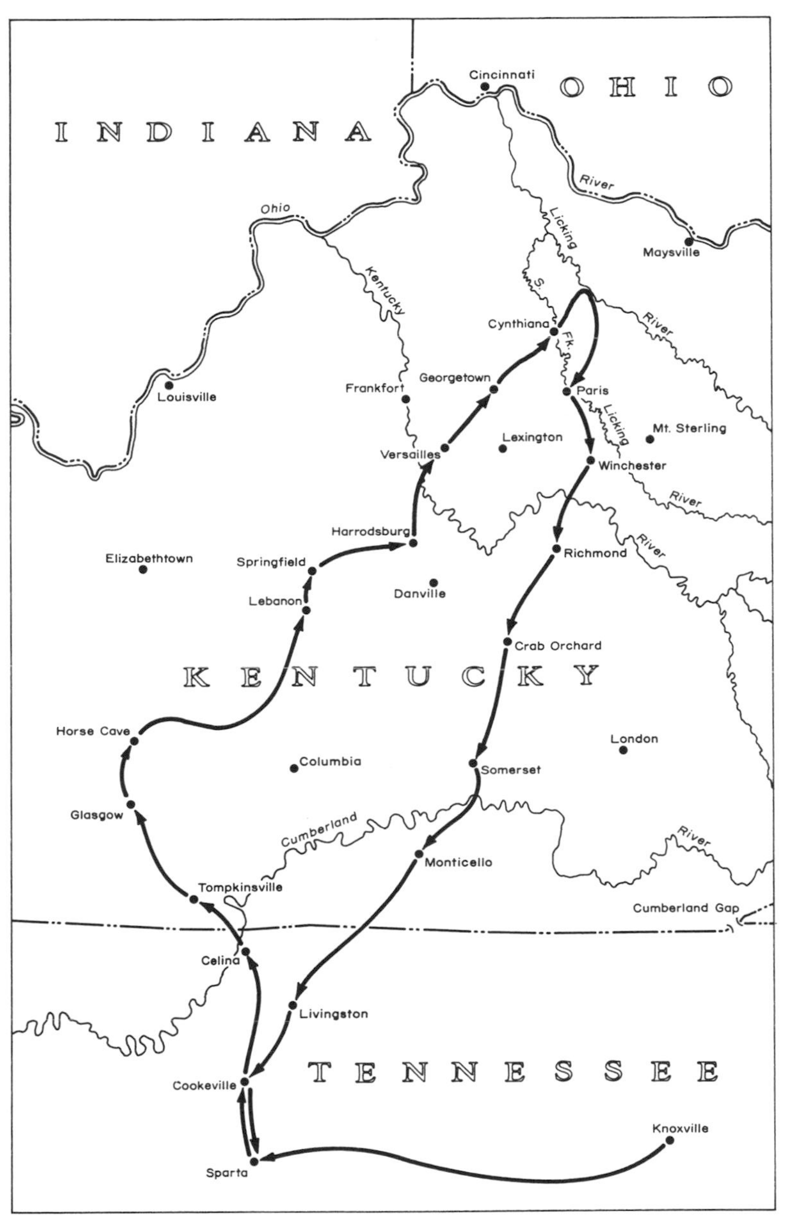

The First Kentucky Raid, July 1862

ate you from despotism of a tyrannical faction and to rescue my native state from the hand of your oppressors." At the end stood this plea: "Greet them with the willing hands of fifty thousand of Kentucky's brave. Their advance is already with you."

After dark, John Castleman and a few others managed to slip through Federal lines into Lexington to visit friends and sweethearts. Castleman also smuggled in a number of copies of Morgan's recruiting posters and placed them in prominent spots about town. As a result, enough men to form a new cavalry company showed up at Georgetown the next day.

Meanwhile, an open letter to Morgan appeared in the *Louisville Journal*. Written by the editor, George Prentice, the message read: "Again we say to you, misguided young man, as much for your own good as ours, and more in mercy than in anger—prodigal, profligate, apostate, traitor, ingrate, and brigand—Go!"

Morgan took Prentice's advice, but not until he had first marched on Cynthiana, a move that may not have been altogether wise, for a strong Federal garrison resisted. Again it was Kentuckians fighting Kentuckians, and the battle at the covered bridge across the Licking River resulted in some of the bitterest fighting yet experienced by Morgan, Shiloh's violence not excepted. When it was over, Morgan counted 8 dead and 28 wounded. He also had captured 300 horses and a number of small arms and had destroyed a large quantity of commissary and medical supplies, tents, guns, and ammunition. As they rode away toward Paris, they carried their dead with them in hastily commandeered wagons and buggies.

Morgan's command spent that night in Paris. There they rounded up 30 or 40 more horses, and the next day, at Winchester, several new recruits were added to the roster. They crossed the Kentucky River and headed for Richmond, where nearly 50 young men were sworn in.

Apparently Morgan's poster was beginning to get results. They reached Somerset on July 22, and Ellsworth cut his ever-faithful telegraph key into the U.S. military telegraph line to Louisville and clicked off a message to Prentice, asking him when he would be home, as Morgan planned to drop by. Here at Somerset the men found a large Federal supply of blankets and shoes. They loaded several wagons with as much as they would hold and destroyed the remainder, along with a number of guns and a supply of ammunition.

The weary but elated group of Raiders crossed the Cumberland River and headed for Monticello, twenty-one miles away. They felt much safer now that the river was behind them, for they were sure that pursuit of some kind had been only hours away. A few days later they reached Livingston, Tennessee; passing through Cookeville, they arrived at Sparta early in August.

Morgan in a report of what historians now call his First Kentucky Raid summed up the results: "I left Knoxville on the 4th day of this month [July] with about nine hundred men, and returned to Livingston on the 28th inst. with nearly twelve hundred, having been absent just 24 days, during which time I have traveled over a thousand miles, captured seventeen towns, destroyed all the government supplies and arms in them, dispersed about fifteen hundred Home Guards and paroled nearly twelve hundred regular troops. I lost in killed, wounded and missing of the number I carried into Kentucky, about ninety."

5

KENTUCKY REVISITED

UPON ARRIVAL AT SPARTA, Morgan's Second Kentucky Cavalry reoccupied their old camp, which, except for an abundance of weeds grown up in their absence, was about as it was when they had left it two months before.

Basil Duke was placed in charge as Morgan rode off for a meeting with his new commanding officer, General Bragg, who had succeeded the ailing Beauregard and established headquarters at Chattanooga. There on July 31 General Edmund Kirby Smith (who had come down on the train from Knoxville), Bragg, and Morgan held a council of war with other officers to map their next move.

The Confederate government at Richmond had been wanting something done about Buell's Federal army, which at the time was casually rebuilding the Memphis & Charleston Railroad track across northern Alabama. The plan they came up with at the Chattanooga conference was a noble one. Its main thrust was designed to oust all Federal forces from Kentucky and Tennessee. As a necessary first step, Buell had to be gotten out of Alabama.

Their proposed attack would be a two-pronged one. Bragg would move northwest across Tennessee, skirt Nashville, and cut Buell's supply line. Smith would head north from Knoxville, cross into Kentucky near Cumberland Gap, and take the rich Bluegrass section, a move that was sure to please the high command at Richmond.

Bragg's strategy was based on his belief that the people of Kentucky had been forced to remain in the Union and, if given the proper opportunity, would rise up to a man and help rout the Federals back across the Ohio River. After Smith had conquered the Bluegrass, Bragg would absorb those "liberated" Kentuckians into his Army of East Tennessee.

While this was going on, Bragg would defeat Buell's army somewhere north of Nashville, perhaps even in the city itself; afterwards he would meet Smith in Frankfort, where they would inaugurate a Confederate governor. Kentucky then would be able to take her rightful place on the roster of Southern states.

Much of the success of this proposed raid into Kentucky would hinge on the ability of Morgan's Second Kentucky Cavalry to perform its usual top-notch hit-and-run tactics. Both Bragg and Smith were impressed with the colonel's account of his first big raid into Kentucky, and now they were giving him another chance to make the kind of contribution his outfit was best suited for.

It was an elated Morgan who returned to Sparta on August 10 with riding orders in his pocket. In a conference that night with Basil Duke and the other officers of his command, he explained their part in the invasion. The first task would be to raid their favorite target, the L & N Railroad, at Gallatin. The purpose would be to cut, once and for all, General Buell's supply line from Louisville. He then sketched briefly what Bragg and Smith planned to do, and he impressed upon his officers that the success of the plan depended upon their luring Buell back northward. Cutting the supply line would do it, he said, and the Second Kentucky Cavalry might thus be able to play a key role in shortening the war.

By daybreak on the morning of August 12 Morgan's

Second Kentucky, augmented the day before by 30 recruits from Kentucky, approached the little town of Gallatin. Through advance intelligence Morgan knew that the town was garrisoned by a force of about 375 Federals. Some of them would be quartered at the fairgrounds; others would be on picket duty at various points in the vicinity, including the railroad depot, adjacent bridges, and the twin tunnels north of town. The attack on Gallatin was swift and sure.

A report written by Albert Fink, the L & N Railroad's engineer and superintendent of machinery and road department at Louisville, described what happened at Gallatin that morning: "On the 12th of August, Morgan took possession of Gallatin, captured Federal forces stationed there, destroyed a train of 29 cars, the water station [apparently replacement of the facility destroyed during his 1861 raid], a bridge two-and-a-half miles south, and another six miles north of Gallatin. He also captured the Federal forces on Tunnel Hill seven miles north of Gallatin."

At Tunnel Hill the track of the L & N runs through two tunnels, both of which are still in use. They were bored through an outcropping of the western edge of the Cumberland Plateau, and the railroad refers to them as the "South Tunnels." "Big South" is nearly a thousand feet long and "Little South" about six hundred; they are separated by less than four hundred feet of open track. These tunnels were dug in the late 1850s through rather porous slate and required heavy timbers to shore up the interiors. On that day in 1862, Morgan decided to wreck "Big South" tunnel. John Castleman, the young officer who had so brilliantly maneuvered his cavalry unit around Lexington during the First Kentucky Raid in July, helped with the wrecking job. In an account written after the war, he said: "We ran a captured freight locomotive inside the longer of the tunnels at high speed and wrecked it upon a pile of cribbed crossties. We then set fire to the ties and to the wood framework [inside]. After it had burned, slate rock collapsed from the roof."

An inspection by Fink some days later indicated that the collapsed roof had contained a vein of coal, which also caught fire and continued to smolder for several days after the tunnel was wrecked. When it was all over, debris twelve feet deep in places, plus a wrecked locomotive, blocked Big South tunnel for over eight hundred feet inside its length.

To make the job complete, Morgan's group en route back down the hill toward Gallatin, ripped up track, built fires with the crossties, heated the rails to a glowing red, then, with men at both ends of a rail length, bent each piece around a nearby tree. "Morgan's neckties," some called them. After setting fire to a building at the fairgrounds, the Raiders headed toward Hartsville, fifteen miles away, for some much-needed rest.

The wrecking of Big South tunnel attracted General Buell's attention just as Bragg had hoped it would. It also stopped the flow of Federal supplies from Louisville. By the last of August, Buell's army had full rations for only ten more days. The railroad made several attempts to reopen the tunnel, but, according to Superintendent Fink, "workmen could not be induced to commence operation without a strong military guard," and such guard could not be obtained because the military situation was so tense.

"Confederates were still present in the area," Fink said, and added: "Reports reached Louisville about the 23rd of August that a large Federal force sent by Buell for the purpose of dislodging Morgan from his position had been defeated near Hartsville, Tenn., and thus our prospects of putting the road again in running order were not very encouraging."

Back in east Tennessee, everything was going according to plan. General Smith had marched out of Knoxville on August 14 with 20,000 men, bound for the Bluegrass State. Within a few days Bragg and Buell, too, would be marching. None of the three generals had any idea of the bloody battle that would engulf them in less than eight weeks.

Bragg, with 30,000 men, marched out of Chattanooga toward Murfreesboro and made a feint toward Nashville. This action, intended to smoke Buell out of his lair in Alabama, succeeded mainly because his supply line was cut. In motion again, Bragg passed east of Nashville and headed toward Glasgow, Kentucky. A few days later, Buell's army, 35,000 strong, marching north at last, camped at Murfreesboro. There he received the news that Kirby Smith had captured over 4,000 Federal troops during a battle with Major General William Nelson at Richmond, Kentucky, and even then was heading for Lexington. Not satisfied with those conquests, Smith's advance forces pressed ahead as far as Covington, a move which thoroughly frightened the city of Cincinnati, that longtime Federal stronghold across the Ohio River. With Confederates at their very gateway, citizens began to fortify the city and sent a hasty plea for help to the governor at Columbus. In less than two weeks Ohio's oddest army, perhaps one of the oddest assembled during the war, in the tradition of the Minutemen sprang 50,000 strong from nowhere to stem the tide of Kirby Smith's forces headed their way. Carrying shotguns, muskets, rifles, pistols, and other assorted weapons, the army was quickly christened the "Squirrel Hunters," and never was known by any other name. They did not fire a shot in anger, but they successfully protected the city from Smith's invasion.

Reaction at Louisville was almost as extreme. Its population of 80,000 packed up belongings in preparation for evacuating the city and fleeing to Indiana.

Buell lost no time in crossing the Cumberland River and heading for Kentucky. With Bragg ahead of him, probably at Bowling Green, he would be in complete control of Buell's supply line. But there was another deepening fear. If Buell did not catch him, Bragg would march right on to Louisville!

Back in Hartsville, after the Raiders had returned from wrecking Big South Tunnel, Lieutenant Gordon E. Niles, the New York newspaperman who had joined Morgan in Chattanooga in May, found a printing press and several cases of type stored in an abandoned building. He rounded up four or five of the Raiders who had typesetting experience and on August 16, published the first issue of a short-lived little newspaper, the *Vidette.* In order to complete his press run, Niles used any kind of paper he could find; thus part of the edition wound up on pink and green wrapping paper. That first issue carried comment on the activities of the Raiders at Gallatin, a lengthy salute to Southern womanhood, and a new poem, "Morgan's War Song, by B. W. D. one of Morgan's men." It also contained a column of military news, troop movements, deeds of Morgan's command, and even some letters from friends. Two issues labeled "Extra" followed, one on the seventeenth and another on the nineteenth. The next day, Niles was killed during an attack on Federals at Edgefield Junction, 10 miles north of Nashville.

R. M. Gano put together the issue published August 24, a single sheet printed on both sides. It contained the obituary of Niles, some of Morgan's general orders, and another poem, "Here's Your Mule." The third numbered issue, dated August 30, was printed in Glasgow, Kentucky, where the Raiders had stopped en route to Lexington to join General Smith. The editor was S. K. Bangs.

Probably no more than two other issues were published—one October 28 at Hopkinsville, Kentucky, and the other November 2 at Springfield, Tennessee. Both were edited by Robert A. Alston, Morgan's adjutant general. The last issue contained four pages and was printed on good quality paper.

Morgan was quite proud of his command's journalistic efforts, even if the paper only came out, as someone said, "semi occasionally." He was so pleased that he published several more of his general orders in it, and to make sure that the Confederate high command was kept informed, he fired off copies to Richmond as soon as they came off the press. A copy also went to George Prentice, pro-Union editor of the *Louisville Journal*, who often bore much of the brunt of the paper's barbed editorial comment.

Only seven different copies of the *Vidette* have ever been found, an indication that it probably did not survive beyond the November 2 issue. Although it had a short life, the paper was unique in the annals of war, a particularly unlikely project for a cavalry unit such as Morgan's.

As Bragg moved slowly into Kentucky, Morgan began stocking up on clothing and military supplies his men would need on their long trip. On August 28 he received a message from Smith ordering the Second Kentucky to meet him in Lexington on September 2. Early the next morning, Morgan's command, 900 strong, marched out of Hartsville. They were the same old enthusiastic bunch—noisy and "full of devilment," as one Hartsville girl smilingly described them, laughing, telling jokes, and singing. This time, they said, they were heading for Kentucky for good. If they ever saw Hartsville again they expected it would be as civilians, for the war would be over soon.

The Second Kentucky did not get to Lexington by September 2, but Kirby Smith did. Morgan was not far away; his command crossed the Kentucky line into Allen County on August 29, reached Glasgow the next day, and then spent two days at Columbia. Proceeding toward Lexington, they passed through Liberty, and camped at Hustonville on September 2. With Lexington so near, and in Confederate hands for a change, enthusiasm ran high. The next morning the entire command was up at dawn with horses saddled and ready to go. The clean smell of late summer bluegrass seemed to give each man that urge to step a little more lively; even the horses moved at a faster clip than usual. By midmorning, they were in Danville and by sundown they had reached Nicholasville—Lexington was just twelve miles away! Many wanted to keep going despite the approaching darkness, but Morgan said No. They were going to clean up, brush and curry their horses, polish their saddles, and put on their best uniforms. "Tomorrow," Morgan told them, "we are going to enter Lexington in parade formation!"

It was 10 A.M. on September 4 when John Hunt Morgan, wearing the full dress uniform of a Confederate colonel, rode smartly into Lexington. Behind him in perfect formation rode his entire command of 900 men. None of the hundreds who began to crowd the sidewalks to watch Morgan ride into the city would recall the little band that had surreptitiously left Lexington with guns hidden in two hay wagons hardly a year before.

All the successful raids Morgan had led, all the newspaper stories written about him, indeed all his exploits combined could not top this moment, filled as it was with the most impressive pomp and circumstance he could muster. Somewhere along the street a band picked up their cadence and marched out in front of them. Morgan saluted smartly as he passed each Confederate flag, and as his command approached the center of town, flags fluttered from almost every window. Friends and Confederate sympathizers now crowded into the streets, cheering, waving, reaching out, touching. Morgan shook as many hands as he could without stopping his columns completely. As he turned off Main

Street, he had difficulty clearing a path through the crowd so he could head for Hopemont.

As the men were dismounting to enjoy the huge welcome, Alston was looking for a printing press to run off a new batch of recruiting posters. "Arouse Kentuckians!" it was headed, and the text contained a personal message from Morgan. Young men flocked into the temporary recruiting station Alston had set up, all wanting to join the cavalry—specifically, Morgan's Second Kentucky. There was no doubt about it; the dropout from Transylvania had indeed come home.

Gifts poured into Hopemont where he was staying. A group of women from the neighborhood brought in his regimental colors, which they had embroidered with their own hands. A delegation of friends brought him a set of silver spurs. But it was Keene Richards, a Bluegrass breeder, whose generosity touched Morgan most. Answering a knock at the door, Morgan discovered a thoroughbred gelding standing on the street in front of Hopemont. "His name is Glencoe and he's yours," Richards said.

By the middle of September, General Buell's army had reached Bowling Green, but there was no trace of Bragg. Scouts moving into the area beyond the Barren River discovered Bragg's army at Munfordville, where the Confederates had surprised and captured a garrison of Federals from Indiana assigned to guard the railroad bridge across Green River. Buell shuddered. His men were hungry, and now Bragg's entire army was between him and Louisville, where warehouses bulged with food and all sorts of supplies. There was nothing left to do but fight. Munfordville, it appeared, would be the site of Kentucky's first major battle of the war. For Buell, the battle was a necessity. For Bragg, it would be his big chance—the first battle of his independent command and his first real opportunity to make Richmond aware of what he could do.

General John Hunt Morgan and Black Bess
Courtesy of *Courier-Journal and Louisville Times*

The fight at the Licking River bridge, Cynthiana, July 1862
Courtesy of L & N Railroad

Raiders bivouacking in the court square, Paris

Courtesy of L & N Railroad

Making L & N track into "Morgan's neckties"
Courtesy of L & N Railroad

Union troops rebuilding Bacon's Creek bridge

Courtesy of L & N Railroad

Twin tunnels on the L & N Railroad
Courtesy of L & N Railroad

THE VIDETTE.

VOL. 1. HARTSVILLE, TENN., AUGUST 16, 1862. NO. 1

Morgan's War-Song.

By R. W. D.,
ONE OF MORGAN'S BRIGADE.

Ye Sons of the South, take your weapons in hand,
For the foot of the foe hath insulted your land!
Sound, sound the loud alarm!
Arise! arise and arm!
Let the hand of each freeman grasp the sword to maintain
Those rights, which, once lost, he can never regain.
Gather fast 'neath our flag, for 'tis God's own decree,
That its folds shall still float o'er a land that is free!

See ye not those strange clouds which now darken the sky?
Hear ye not that stern thunder, now bursting so nigh?
Shout, shout your battle cry!
Win, win this fight or die!
To your country devote every life that she gave,—
Let the land they invade give their army its grave!
Gather fast 'neath our flag, for 'tis God's own decree,
That its folds shall still float o'er a land that is free!

On our hearts, and our cause, and our God we rely;
And a nation shall rise, or a people shall die!
Form, form the serried line,—
Advance our proud ensign.
What our fathers achieved our own valor can keep,
And we'll save our fair land, or we'll sleep our last sleep!
Gather fast 'neath our flag, for 'tis God's own decree,
That its folds shall still float o'er a land that is free!

Tho' their plunder paid hosts come to ravage our land,—
Give our fields to the spoiler, our homes to the brand,
Our souls are all aglow,
To face the hireling foe,
Give the robbers to know that we never will yield,
While the arm of one Southron a weapon can wield.
Gather fast 'neath our flag, for 'tis God's own decree,
That its folds shall still wave o'er a land that is free!

From our far Southern shore now arises a prayer,—
The cry of our women fills with anguish the air.
Oh! list that pleading voice!
Each youth now make his choice,—
Now tamely submit, like a coward and slave,
Or rise and resist, like the free and the brave!
Gather fast 'neath our flag, for 'tis God's own decree,
That its folds shall still float o'er a land that is free!

Kentucky! Kentucky! can you suffer the sight,
Of your sisters insulted?—your friends in the fight?
Awake! be free again!
Oh! break the tyrant's chain!
Seize the sword you once drew but to strike for the right,
From the homes of our fathers drive the dastard in flight.
Gather fast 'neath our flag, for 'tis God's own decree,
That its folds shall still float o'er a land that is free!

KNOXVILLE, Tenn., July 3, 1862.

The Women of the South.

The soldiers of the Confederacy, although fighting in the noblest cause, and for the highest stake that men ever battled for, have during the long and unequal conflict had much to [illegible] them. Half fed and illy clad, they have been compelled to endure the rigor of a winter campaign in a climate to them alike unnatural and inhospitable. They have had to encounter the exhausting heat of a southern summer, deprived of all those appliances which secure either health or comfort. While their enemy has been bounteously provided with all the material of war, with all that medical science [illegible] to save life or alleviate suffering, with all that money and access to the markets of the world could supply to make war easy, the southern patriot shut out from all sources whence could come any such assistance, has had to struggle on through the gloomy scenes of hardship and disasters which have hitherto characterized this war, to him supported only by the indomitable fortitude with which the [illegible] of his cause and the magnitude of the interests involved could give him. But amid all the trials of the dreadful struggle he has had one unfailing [illegible] of cheer—the sympathy which the noble daughters of the South have extended to the defenders of their land—it is not too much to say that but for the heroic spirit—the self-sacrifice—the generous devotion which they have displayed, the fight would ere now have been ended and lost. Every impulse of the southern heart has been fired, every manly characteristic of the Southern [illegible] has been strengthened by the conduct of their women.

The chivalry they have inherited from Knightly ancestors—the holy love they bear to wife, to mother and to sister—the duty which they owe to those who have nursed them through the pangs of wounds and sickness and cheered them with high and holy encouragement upon the [illegible] march, and ever on the eve of battle, have appealed to those [illegible] which [illegible] once aroused, make men invincible.

Let the soldiers who survive this contest [illegible] a life-long gratitude to the glorious beings who deprived themselves of comforts to minister to their necessities, and when the sound of war is hushed, and our people [illegible] its terrible dangers only as [illegible] let the Confederacy not forget to accord its highest honors to those who when its existence was [illegible] for [illegible] [illegible] [illegible] [illegible] [illegible] so much to achieve it.

A COMPLETE SURPRISE—GALLATIN TAKEN—COL. BOONE WITH 200 MEN TAKEN PRISONERS—UNCONDITIONALLY SURRENDERED—THE RAIL-ROAD BRIDGE AND TUNNEL DESTROYED, &c.

On Sunday August 12th Col. MORGAN'S command left Sparta. On Tuesday morning at 4½ A. M. it entered Gallatin 75 miles distant. The pickets behind whom we gained the turnpike were captured without either noise or resistance. Col. Boone commanding the Federal force, was made a prisoner at the Hotel under the same convenient circumstances. The entire Confederate force marched through Gallatin to within less than half a mile of the Fair Grounds where the Federals were encamped before the latter were apprised of their presence and the information was then conveyed them by a flag of truce, accompanied with a demand for their unconditional surrender.

When the bearers of the flag, two in number came in sight of the camp ground, they found their appearance a cause of much surprise and confusion the long-roll was beaten, the troops crowded in to the amphitheatre and a Babel of tongues, among which the *Teutonic* was strikingly conspicuous betrayed, how unwelcome was their presence.

Col. Boone having surrendered, however, his officers were too courteous and subordinate not to follow and endorse his example, thus Gallatin was won without a shot.

The bridge below town was burned, the magnificent tunnel six miles above, surrendered by its guard, was completely destroyed, and when Col MORGAN left the town, it was with the knowledge that he had rendered that Rail Road useless to the Yankees for either supplies or a retreat.

HARTSVILLE, TENN., Aug. 15, 1862.
GEN'L JNO. H. MORGAN,
Commanding Brigade, Sir:

On the morning of the 12th inst., when within 2 miles of Gallatin I was ordered to accompany the squad of men under command of CAPT. DESHEA, who were sent in for the purpose of taking Col. Boone prisoner, which was accomplished by the gallant Captain in fine style. I immediately proceeded to the Rail Road Depot where I understood the Telegraph office was, as well as the operator. I at once bursted in the door and running up stairs found the operator in bed staring into the barrel of my six shooter. He surrendered and accompanied me down stairs into the operating room. He soon made me acquainted with the signals of the line &c., when I tested the line and found the wire O. K. to Nashville and also to Louisville, this was about 4 minutes 40 seconds A. M., and the office Hours are not until 7 minutes 30 seconds therefore between, the Hours of 5 and 7 there were no operators in their offices on the line, at 7 and 10 the operator at Nashville, in the Depot Office called me and reported the train leaving on time, as also did the operator at Franklin. I informed Capt. McCann who was at the depot about the time that train from the North would be at Gallatin. He accordingly made arrangements to take charge of the train and no sooner had it arrived at the water tank than he did so.

The train from Nashville was now over due, I enquired of the Nashville operator as follows:

"Train No. 6, not yet arrived; what can be the trouble with her. He replied:

"Guess Morgan's got her, she left on time with 27 cars [illegible].

Nashville, Bowling-Green called me and asked about the train from Nashville. I told him not yet arrived this was about 9 oclock.

Bowling Green then called Nashville saying to Her, "Gallatin says No. 6 not arrived have you heard from them. Nashville replied no. They left on time.

Bowling-Green to Nashville, any rumors of an enemy between Gallatin and Nashville.

Nashville to Bowling-Green, nary rumor.

Nashville called me and informed me that, the passenger train bound North had left on time.

Enquiry after enquiry was made of me as to these two trains that left Nashville on time.

Everything passed off without suspicion until 10 o'clock 45 minutes A. M. when Nashville commenced calling me with a gusto sufficient to induce me to believe that the trains had returned and our occupation of Gallatin made known in Nashville, but I was on the alert to counteract this report, and did not answer the Nashville operator until I could get Mr. Brooks, the Federal Operator in the office who was under guard outside the office. I required Mr Brooks to answer all questions as knowing the Nashville Operator would try and ask me a question I could not answer something pertaining to past events.

Accordingly Mr. Brooks answered the call when the following conversation ensued:

Nashville to Gallatin, what was the name of that young lady that you accompanied to Major Foster's?

Gallatin to Nashville, I don't remember of going to Major Foster's with any young lady.

Nashville to Gallatin, What about that Nitric Acid I sent you the other day.

Gallatin to Nashville, you sent me no Nitric Acid.

Nashville to Gallatin, Mr. Marshal the Superintendent of the Rail Road is not yet satisfied but that you are Morgan's Operator and he wishes you to tell him who you wished to take your place while you were gone on leave of absence, how long you wished to be gone, and when did you wish to go?

Gallatin to Nashville, Tell Mr. Marshall I wished Mr. Clayton to take my place while I got a weeks leave to go to Cincinnati.

I informed Mr. Brooks before I gave him my place at the instrument, that I should listen to his replies to any enquiries that might be made of him, and I threatened to carry him to Dixie if the replies did not satisfy the Nashville Operator.

I am (as well as Mr. Brooks), happy to say that the Nashville Operator was perfectly satisfied and as the train bound South was now at Gallatin waiting for the trains bound North, the Superintendent of the Road wished it to move to Edgefield Junction, and there meet and pass the trains bound North and accordingly he sent the following message:

NASHVILLE, Aug. 12th, 1862.
To MURPHY, Conductor,
Gallatin, Tenn.

You will run to Edgefield Junction to meet and pass trains No. 4 and 6 and pass them both at that point. Answer how you understand.

B. MARSHALL.

I gave Murphy's reply understanding the order as above.

Nashville then said trains No. 4 and 6 left at 11:15.

During the afternoon dispatches were passing to and fro but none of them in relation to any enemy and no suspicion was yet attached to me being in the Gallatin office.

The enemy not knowing of your whereabouts the dispatches were of no benefit or interest to us and I copied but few. About 4 o'clock the Nashville operator called and informed me that they had positive information of our occupation of Gallatin. He said the trains had returned the second time and had brought reliable information beyond doubt, and enquired what had become of Murphy and his train but I gave him no satisfactory reply About 5 o'clock I sent your dispatch which was as follows:

GALLATIN, Aug. 12th, 1862.
To GEO. D. PRENTICE,
Louisville, Ky.

Your prediction in yesterday's paper regarding my whereabouts is like most of the items from your pen. You had better go over to Jeffersonville to sleep to-night.

JOHN H. MORGAN.
Com. Brigade.

The following is a dispatch I sent to Prentice for a lady who was in the office at Gallatin:

GALLATIN, Aug. 12th, 1862.
GEO. D. PRENTICE,
Louisville, Ky.

Your friend, Col. John H. Morgan, and his brave followers are enjoying the hospitalities of this town to-day. Wouldn't you like to be here? The Colonel has seen your $100,000 reward for his head, and offers $100,000 better for yours, at short range.

Wash Morgan, whom you published in your paper sometime ago when he was at Knoxville, accompanies his cousin John with 400 Indians. He seeks no scalp but yours.

A SECESH LADY.

The above is respectfully submitted.
I am your obedient servant,
GEO. A. ELSWORTH.
Telegraph Operator.

First issue of Morgan's newspaper
Courtesy of Southern Historical Collection,
University of North Carolina

General John Hunt Morgan
Courtesy of L & N Railroad

On the evening of September 20, Buell issued orders to prepare for an attack on Bragg at Munfordville the next morning. But before Buell could get his men in battle formation that morning, scouts informed him that they were facing only Bragg's rear guard. The remainder of the 30,000-man army had disappeared. Quickly pushing the rear guard aside, Buell began his march to Louisville, arriving there on the twenty-ninth.

But what about Bragg? Many strategists since have wondered what was in his mind. As one of his own men put it: "He had Buell in the hollow of his hand, then he just moved over and let him pass."

Bragg, for some reason of his own that he never did fully explain, left Munfordville and headed toward Bardstown despite the fact that Morgan had helped to avert an attack by Federals from Louisville by burning the big railroad bridge across Salt River at Shepherdsville. Historian Stanley Horn would say years later, "In a negative way General Bragg's failure to fight . . . was one of the great crises of the Civil War—probably its greatest moral crisis."

After a leisurely eight-day stay at Bardstown, Bragg left General Polk in charge and moved on to Lexington. Then, as planned, he and Kirby Smith rode to Frankfort on October 4 and watched as Richard Hawes was installed as Confederate governor of Kentucky. In his inaugural address Hawes assured the people that Kentucky would be held by the Confederates no matter what the cost. But even as he spoke those words, one of Buell's advance columns was nearing Frankfort, and within a few hours the entire inaugural party had fled, leaving the capital at the mercy of the enemy. With that move, the Confederate territory that had been so boldly carved from Kentucky's famed Bluegrass region by Kirby Smith slowly but surely began to fall apart.

Morgan knew it would be only a matter of time until Buell found Bragg—unless the Confederate general turned immediately and fled toward Tennessee. While there was still time to make a sane appraisal of their actions, Morgan held a conference with Basil Duke. They agreed that they had accomplished their part of the campaign to conquer Kentucky, as had Kirby Smith. Some officers of Morgan's command said it was Bragg who had not completed his part of the overall strategy. Others seemed to think that Bragg had lost his nerve at Munfordville, and rather than face Buell, he had turned in the dark of night and fled to Bardstown.

Buell's army, now fully rested and strengthened by reinforcements and a twenty-mile-long supply train from Louisville, was lumbering along in a three-pronged advance toward the Bluegrass. As the impact of Buell's full-scale advance struck Bragg and Smith, Bragg made plans to try to outmaneuver the Federal general. In spite of earlier warnings from some of his own officers, Bragg had scattered his army over at least six counties. Some were still at Bardstown; others were at Lawrenceburg, Versailles, Bryantsville, and Perryville. Morgan and Duke, along with several of the Raiders, watched as Hardee's Corps of Smith's army left Lexington and moved southwest on the Nicholasville Road toward Harrodsburg and Danville. The day was October 6, 1862. Lexington was witnessing the hustle and organized confusion of an army preparing for battle, and never again would it see such a large concentration of troops, Confederate or Federal.

Morgan's Second Kentucky, under the overall command of youthful "Fighting Joe" Wheeler, moved into a screening position to protect Hardee's rear. At about the same time, approximately ten miles southwest of Harrodsburg in the vicinity of the village of Perryville, Bragg's pickets had blundered into a similar group from Buell's army.

It was at Perryville on October 8, in the area of Doctor's Creek and Chaplin Hills, that Kentucky's first and only major action of the war got under way. The action of this unplanned battle was as agonizing and as bloody as Shiloh, but Morgan's Raiders were not there. With permission from General Smith to select his own route of departure from Kentucky, Morgan made a quick, vigorous raid on Federal forces pressing toward Lexington; then the Second Kentucky raced away toward the west. Now about 1,800 strong, they attacked one of Buell's wagon trains on the Louisville turnpike, ransacking and burning all but two of the vehicles. They loaded these with supplies and resumed their march. At Elizabethtown they stopped a troop train on the L & N Railroad, and put it out of commission. Then they galloped off toward Leitchfield. On the twenty-second they crossed the Green River at Morgantown and stopped at Greenville for the night, sleeping in the snow. En route back to Tennessee, they swung by Hopkinsville to visit Colonel Thomas G. Woodward, Morgan's old friend who was camped there with a cavalry unit composed chiefly of men from Christian and Trigg counties. Hopkinsville was definitely pro-Confederate, and Morgan's command was welcomed with open arms.

From Hopkinsville Colonel Gano was sent with his regiment to damage the railroad between Bowling Green and Gallatin, as well as part of the Memphis Branch in the vicinity of Russellville. He set to work, first on the L & N, by burning the bridges over Whippoorwill and Elk Fork creeks and a bridge three-and-a-half miles north of Russellville. He also destroyed a portion of the track between Bowling Green and Gallatin on the main line to Nashville. Moving over to the Edgefield & Kentucky Railroad, Gano's men burned a trestle near Springfield, Tennessee. The next day they destroyed a trestle near Ridgetop, the peak where the railroad starts downgrade south of Springfield, and three small bridges between Ridgetop and Goodletsville. The Federals would now have as difficult a time getting out of Kentucky by rail as they had getting in.

Meanwhile, Morgan's main force left Hopkinsville November 1 and crossed into Tennessee, joining Gano's regiment at Springfield. After a futile attempt to burn a concentration of nearly 300 freight cars stored on tracks at Edgefield on the north side of the Cumberland River at Nashville, the Raiders moved on to a point four miles from Lebanon. There was a reason why Morgan chose that particular location. It was not far from Murfreesboro. Martha Ready lived there, and she and Morgan were still in love.

6

CHRISTMAS 1862

IN EARLY DECEMBER, direct from running interference for General Bragg in Kentucky, Morgan and his Raiders were back at Murfreesboro. Buell's army had returned to Nashville, but without its testy commander. Because of his reluctance to pressure Bragg during his withdrawal from Perryville, Buell had been relieved of his command and the assignment given to General William S. Rosecrans.

Bragg's army had straggled into Murfreesboro on November 20 and 21. Within little more than a two-day march to the west was Rosecrans and the Federal army, also going into winter camp.

As Bragg's army began to set up their tents, Morgan was bustling about with plans of his own. He explained to the general that his scouts probing in the vicinity of Hartsville, forty miles north of Murfreesboro, had discovered a Federal storehouse loaded with supplies. Despite the fact that a contingent of 2,500 Federals stood guard, Morgan assured Bragg that he could capture it.

That was only one of his plans. A week after the raid on Hartsville was over, he planned to marry Miss Martha Ready.

With 1,250 men Morgan rode off toward Hartsville on that cold, blustery morning of December 7, 1862. From the window of her parlor, Mattie Ready watched. "By the grace of God, one day I hope to call myself the wife of John Morgan," she once had confided to a friend. Now, with the wedding just a week away, she could only pray that God's grace was still with her.

Through freezing cold that made travel difficult and most unpleasant, the men took turns, some walking and some riding. At Hartsville, the Federals put up a determined resistance, but with his usual Kentucky luck Morgan quickly scored another victory. In addition to 2,000 prisoners, he captured several wagonloads of supplies, including hundreds of pairs of excellently made shoes and boots, sorely needed by the Confederate soldiers. He also took back to Murfreesboro two artillery pieces that became a permanent part of his battle equipment. These would be with him when he crossed the Ohio River in 1863 to take the war to Yankeeland.

Back in camp at Murfreesboro there was great rejoicing, and the Hartsville Raid was talked of as being the most brilliant of Morgan's entire career. Every man who participated was justifiably proud of the way it had been carried out despite the severe winter weather. Even General Bragg, who never had been one of Morgan's greatest admirers, in a congratulatory message wrote: "The intelligence, zeal and gallantry displayed by [Morgan and Colonel Hunt] will serve as an example and an incentive to still more honorable deeds. To the other brave officers and men composing the expedition, the general tenders his cordial thanks and congratulations."

On Friday after the Hartsville raid, a special train arrived from Chattanooga. The next morning the Murfreesboro *Daily Rebel Banner* carried an item headed "ARRIVAL OF THE PRESIDENT," reporting that "Mr. Davis reached our city last evening and occupied quarters at the residence of Mr. Lewis Maney."

Bragg's army was astir early Saturday preparing for a full-scale presidential review. During that event President Davis announced promotions for a number of the officers in the command. Among them were Morgan, promoted to brigadier general, and Basil Duke, to full colonel.

Morgan was pleased with his new rank but the important event as far as he was concerned took place the next day, Sunday, December 14, when he and Martha Ready were married in the big parlor of the Ready residence. The entire house was profusely decorated with Christmas greens—mistletoe, holly wreaths, and cedar boughs festooned with ropes of popcorn and tinsel or adorned with wax angels. A huge, lavishly decorated cedar Christmas tree stood at one end of the room. Leonidas Polk, wearing the full dress uniform of a Confederate general, slipped the robes of an Episcopal bishop over it to perform the ceremony. Morgan's attendants included Colonel Horace Ready, brother of the bride and member of Hardee's staff, and Colonel George St. Leger Grenfell of Morgan's own staff. Present for the event was one of the most important assemblages of top Confederate brass seen outside of Richmond up to that time. Four generals were there—Bragg, Hardee, Cheatham, and Breckinridge—and a host of lower ranking officers.

One other important person was there, according to Basil Duke, who wrote an account of the affair in 1867. In addition to the generals, he said, "the Commander-in-Chief" also attended.

Debate continues to this day about whether or not Davis attended Morgan and Mattie's wedding. Davis was in Murfreesboro on that Sunday. This is verified by a letter he wrote Mrs. Davis from Chattanooga on the fifteenth in which he said: "Went to Murfreesboro on the 12th and leave today for Mississippi. The troops at Murfreesboro were in fine spirits and well supplied," he said. "Last night on my arrival here [night of December 14] a telegram announced the attack made at Fredericksburg. . . ."

Davis had traveled from Chattanooga to Murfreesboro

on the Nashville & Chattanooga Railroad. Inasmuch as the Federals were in control at Nashville, all northbound trains stopped and turned around at Murfreesboro. With the review on Saturday and the wedding on Sunday, the president's train probably left shortly after Morgan and Mattie's vows were exchanged.

No doubt the events of that busy weekend in Murfreesboro were reported in the *Daily Rebel Banner*, but only two copies of that newspaper are known to survive—the one dated December 13, which announced the arrival of the president, and another dated December 18, which contained no mention of either of the affairs. The only other newspaper account was in the December 17 issue of the *Nashville Daily Union:* "We have been kindly furnished the following item of interest from a source of undoubted veracity and reliability. Jeff Davis reviewed the Confederate forces at Murfreesboro on Saturday last and left on the evening of the same day for Mobile with the intention of visiting the Army of the Mississippi. John Morgan was promoted to the rank of brigadier general and married Sunday night by General Bishop Polk, to Miss Alice, daughter of Hon. Chas. Ready of Murfreesboro."

The *Union*'s source passed along at least two errors. First, instead of heading for Mobile, Davis and his aide returned to Chattanooga on Sunday night. And second, Morgan married Martha Ready, not her sister Alice.

If Davis did not attend the wedding he certainly missed a big celebration. After the ceremony "a great supper was served," so one account stated, "that included huge quantities of roast turkey and duck, boiled ham, fried chicken, venison, other wild game and all the delicacies and good dishes a Southern kitchen can produce. There was also plenty of choice spirits available from Colonel Ready's fine wine cellar."

Three different regimental bands played during the evening, and one came inside after the huge repast and played for dancing. The celebration continued for hours as jokes were told, songs were sung, and toasts proposed. Outside, Morgan's command gathered around campfires and celebrated the occasion in their own individual ways as much of the tribulation of war was forgotten.

Some of Morgan's officers opposed his marriage to Miss Ready. Their reasoning was that it would dampen the general's enthusiasm for riding off across the countryside and raiding where fancy might dictate. Most likely now, they said, the general would want to spend his time in Tennessee rather than to lead raids into Kentucky, burning railroad trestles and perhaps stopping over at some town that was home to many of the Raiders. But those who knew Morgan well had little apprehension that a mere wedding would prevent him from carrying out his assignments against the Federals, and those serving in his command who may have been expecting a long, cozy winter in camp at Murfreesboro would soon be having some second thoughts.

A council of war somewhat like the one held in Chattanooga before the First Kentucky Raid was held in the Ready residence shortly after the wedding. Intelligence reports indicated that General Rosecrans was rapidly stockpiling supplies at Nashville, apparently in preparation for a strong offensive, probably by early spring. His principal supply line, the only one of any consequence besides the secondary one furnished by the river, was the railroad between Louisville and the Tennessee capital, now back in service with the South Tunnel cleared. The Confederate generals surmised that a raid north into Kentucky might be just the thing needed to cut that supply line and thus prevent Rosecrans from sustaining a campaign, either winter or spring. Spies who had been scouting Kentucky in some depth came back with reports that the Federals had built either strong blockhouses or stockades at practically every bridge and tunnel along the entire length of the railroad. Any of these could be captured without too much difficulty, but probably the most likely spot for a major strike at the railroad would be at Muldraugh's Hill about thirty-five miles south of Louisville. Located on the steep grade were two high wood trestles, the largest anywhere along the line. These huge structures were guarded by Federals from behind stockades; but if they could be destroyed, it was estimated that the Federal rail supply line would be cut for much of the winter.

Morgan assured the general that it would be a comparatively simple task to slip into Kentucky and burn those trestles. The tricky part would be getting his men safely back to Tennessee after the trestles had been destroyed.

With Bragg's blessings Morgan assembled his army and moved to Alexandria, Tennessee, twenty-five miles northeast of Murfreesboro as his point of embarkation. On December 21 men and horses received the kind of going-over that always preceded a journey of such magnitude, with some additional attention to details of spit-and-polish in preparation for inspection.

On this particular date, it was more than an inspection; it was a full-scale regimental review, something that Morgan had never held before. In the reviewing stand with the general was his bride of a week and several of his staff officers with their wives. It was one of those rare December days that occasionally brighten that part of Tennessee—pleasant with the sun shining warm against a bare leafless landscape.

Lieutenant James McCreary long remembered that brilliant Sunday. "Company after company moved forward into line with horses prancing, firearms glistening, bugles blowing, and flags waving. . . . It was a grand and imposing scene." Nearly four thousand men marched in review, seven regiments in all. Never before had Morgan commanded so great a number, nor would he ever again.

The next morning, in the same bright December weather, General Morgan kissed his bride goodbye and sent her under special military escort back to Murfreesboro. Mattie Morgan understood that her husband had to leave because duty called. What she did not understand, though, was why he could not promise to be back in Murfreesboro by the twenty-sixth in time for her Christmas ball. It would be the biggest event in that part of Tennessee, and now it appeared that the general wasn't going to be present.

Morgan watched until the buggy bearing his wife disappeared around a curve in the road; then he passed the word to Basil Duke, still his right hand man—*Forward March!* The men marched smartly away toward Kentucky, to carry out what would later be called Morgan's Christmas Raid.

By nightfall on the twenty-third, the Raiders crossed into Kentucky near Tompkinsville in Monroe County. Cheer after cheer resounded through the ranks, and Lieutenant McCreary echoed the sentiments of other Kentuckians in the regiment when he wrote in his diary: "Tonight we are camped on the sacred soil of Kentucky, and it fills my heart with joy and pride."

On Christmas Eve the command continued their thrust into the Bluegrass State, but the sunshine had disappeared, wind cut briskly across their faces, and the sky began to darken. By afternoon they approached the town of Glasgow, where they were the victors in a brush with a group of Federals stationed there. Then somewhere on the Louisville Pike they met a Federal sutler's wagon, described by one of the officers as "the biggest wagon in Kentucky." It was loaded with an enormous supply of Christmas delicacies, including cakes, cookies, and candy. The driver turned out to be an unwilling Santa Claus, but the contents of the wagon helped the men of Morgan's command to have a bit more cheer on that Christmas Eve in an unexpectedly cold and hostile Kentucky.

The first real Federal resistance was experienced on Christmas Day at Bear Wallow, only a few miles from

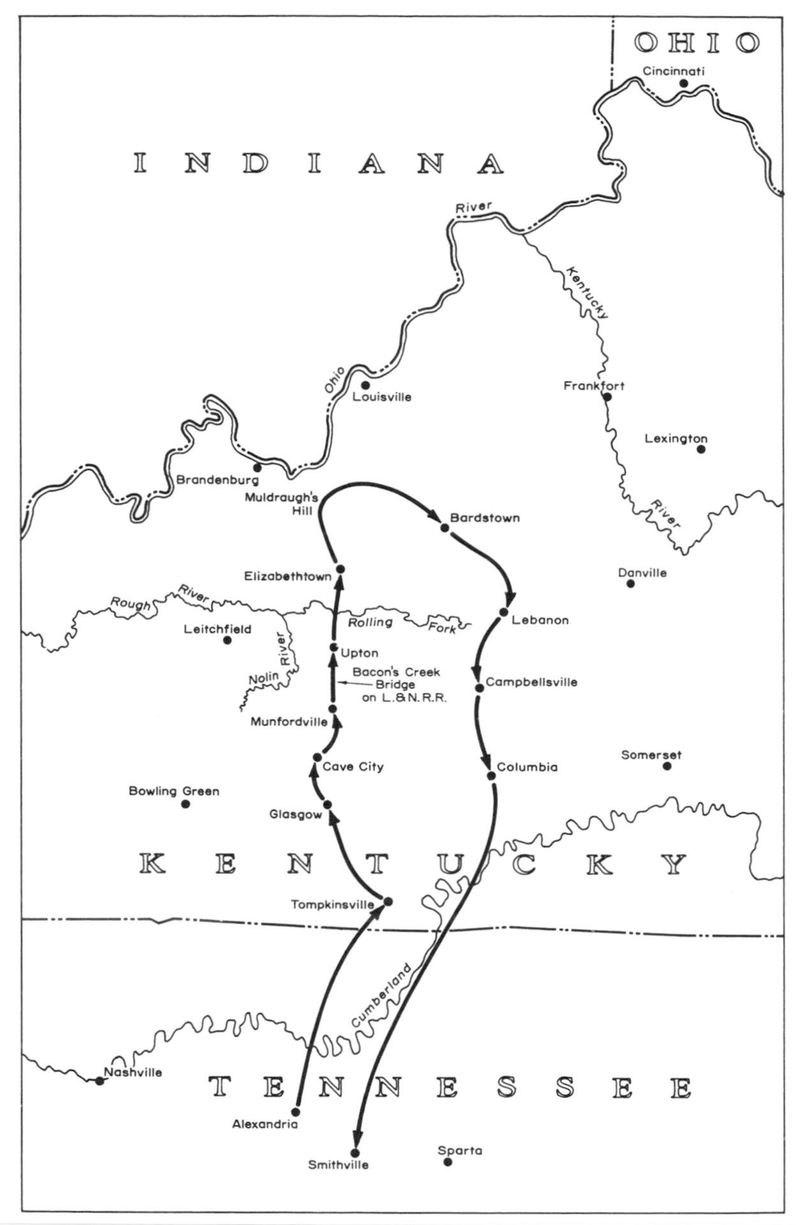

THE CHRISTMAS RAID, 1862-1863

Cave City; but that was soon dispensed with, and the Raiders moved on across Green River. That night they made camp in a chilling rain at a point just a few miles from Upton, a small village on the railroad north of Munfordville. A Union stockade and blockhouse guarded the track there, and to keep the Federals inside from suspecting that his main objective was the big Muldraugh trestles, the next morning Morgan sent a detachment back some six miles to burn the bridge across Bacon's Creek. Upon arrival the men launched an attack on the small garrison of approximately 100 men who were fortified in the nearby blockhouse. The fight was fierce but brief, and even while the men inside were signaling surrender, the "arson brigade" was already at work setting fire to the bridge. Despite the rain, with the help of a brisk wind the crackling blaze soon enveloped the wood structure, and Rosecrans's supply line had received its first break. On the way back to camp, the detachment threw in a little extra effort by tearing up the track and setting fire to piles of crossties for almost the entire distance.

After "Lightning" Ellsworth had cut his key into the telegraph wire and sent messages up and down the line telling of Morgan's plans, both real and fictitious, the Raiders broke camp at Upton and rode out along the railroad track, laughing and joking with the same utter lack of discipline as in the old days. On the way, they wrecked culverts and cattle guards, tearing up vast sections of track, "just to keep in practice," as one man said. At Nolin River, where another blockhouse was located, the bridge was fired and the garrison overcome in less time than it had taken at Bacon's Creek.

With all this activity, Morgan had little time to think about missing his wife's ball that night.

The morning of the twenty-seventh dawned cold but with a clearing sky, and Morgan and his regiment rode away toward Elizabethtown. At the Hardin County seat a garrison of 650 Federals set up a strong resistance, just as Morgan had expected. For protection they had fortified a number of brick warehouses near the railroad station, complete with loopholes through which they could aim rifles. Upon arrival Morgan threw a cordon about the town and placed his artillery pieces on a hill that commanded a clear view of the entire area. From that vantage point shells were lobbed into the Federal stronghold. The bombardment, along with a quick Raider "cavalry" charge on foot along the streets, soon convinced the enemy that Morgan meant business, and they surrendered.

By midafternoon Morgan had set up a temporary headquarters at Elizabethtown and was receiving visitors. Many came because they were sympathetic to the Southern cause. Others, learning that the Confederate commander who made the raid was John Hunt Morgan, stopped by just to see the man upon whom the newspapers of the country had lavished so much attention. Between visits from the local dignitaries, Morgan and his officers were busy checking maps. It was quite evident that the Muldraugh trestles, the big targets for which they had ridden all the way from Tennessee to wreck, were only five short miles away!

December 28, another important Sunday, Morgan and his regiment marched away from Elizabethtown with only one thought—to wreck the Muldraugh trestles. Muldraugh's Hill is actually a rugged range of hills that extends from the Ohio River in the vicinity of present-day Fort Knox some forty or fifty miles in a southeasterly direction across Kentucky. When the railroad was built, the formation was the most formidable barrier along the route south of Louisville. The track makes the climb from the floor of the valley to the top of the hill, a rise of some four hundred feet, in a distance of less than five miles. The two trestles were located about midway up the hill.

Morgan's command made a leisurely march along the track running north of Elizabethtown, "destroying it thoroughly," a report said. They moved on through a deep cut beyond the top of the hill, rounded a curve, and then came out into the open. There, a few hundred yards below them, stood their targets!

Each structure was guarded by its own garrison, and Morgan assigned a brigade to capture each one. The more than 600 Federals, secure behind the walls of their blockhouses, refused Morgan's generous surrender terms; and so the fight began. Soon the artillery was rolled into position, and the battle raged for more than two hours. Shell after shell pounded the stockade and splintered great gaping holes in the walls.

Just as at Bacon's Creek, Nolin River, and Elizabethtown, surrender flags eventually began to wave, and the shelling and rifle fire stopped. Minutes later, torches were eagerly applied to both trestles. Each structure was approximately five hundred feet long and eighty feet high, and the two together contained wood sufficient to make an enormous fire. Smoke began to roll high into the sky; then flames licked upward, higher and higher, until the decking began to smoke from the intense heat. Soon both structures were ablaze from top to bottom and from end to end. Morgan's men, who loved to watch fires, sat back then and enjoyed perhaps the most spectacular blaze they had ever set. Several hours were required to complete the job, but by the time Morgan was ready to pass the word to march, the Muldraugh trestles were only a heap of ashes. In their place were two huge gaps in Rosecrans's rail supply line. All the Raiders had to do now was to get back to Tennessee.

The next day they were in Bardstown, but certainly a group of 4,000 Confederate troops moving that far into Kentucky had not gone unnoticed by the Federals. Their whereabouts was no longer a secret, and even as they prepared to leave Bardstown, a Federal force under the command of Colonel John M. Harlan was headed in their direction. Another force was reported to be assembling at Lebanon to block their departure route—if they could find it. And the two groups of Federals that Morgan had bypassed on the way into Kentucky were known to be marching out of Munfordville and Glasgow. Thus the remaining days of the now famed Christmas Raid might be rather hectic. In the earlier raids, Morgan had been commanding a much smaller group of men. At a moment's notice such a group could quickly cross hills and valleys, ford streams, and hide in the woods to elude pursuers; but with 4,000 men, such tactics were not possible.

Adding to other difficulties, a swirling snowstorm struck the area on the night of December 30, about the time the Raiders began their long march back toward Tennessee. Many of the men who made that bone-chilling ride recalled years later that in their flight they encountered the worst weather experienced during the entire war. Keeping on the trail was most difficult, mainly because of the intense darkness. The snow turned to an icy rain that froze the riders' boots to the stirrups, and the blowing sleet stung their faces and hands as they moved at snail's pace through the bitter cold and miserable night. "When dawn came," one rider said, "our columns looked more like an army of ghosts. All of us, including our horses, were coated with a sheet of ice."

The night of the thirty-first, they reached Campbellsville, but no one felt like staging a celebration or staying up to see the New Year in. The Raiders had been continuously in the saddle, with the exception of two brief rest stops, for over thirty-six hours, and now, with the feeling that they had safely evaded their Federal pursuers, Morgan ordered a halt and set up camp for the night.

The bedraggled columns were en route to Columbia the afternoon of New Year's Day, when they heard a faint but distinct booming sound, almost like thunder. Some said it *was* thunder. To Morgan, Basil Duke, and other officers of the command, the sound was more ominous; they were pretty sure it was the booming of cannon. Where those cannon were, they could not be sure; but if their fears were correct, they were from somewhere in the vicinity of Murfreesboro, seventy-five miles away.

They crossed the state line into Tennessee, and for once, even the Kentuckians in the command were glad to be leaving their beloved state. On January 5 the regiment rode into Smithville, Tennessee, the official terminating point of the Christmas Raid.

Morgan took stock. They had been gone two weeks, during which time they had thrown a good scare into the Federals; the railroad was a wreck from Upton almost to Shepherdsville; nearly 2,000 prisoners were captured as well as a vast quantity of enemy supplies; and his men, thanks to the raids on various Federal supply dumps, were better armed, better clothed, and better mounted than they had been when they left Tennessee. The general's losses were incredibly light—2 killed, 24 wounded, and 64 missing; and he expected that many of the missing would eventually straggle back to camp. They always did.

The railroad, in a brief announcement about the raid a few days later, said: "Morgan . . . struck our road at Bacon's Creek . . . and swept over [it] almost to Shepherdsville. . . . Destroyed were 2,290 feet of bridging, three depots, three water stations, a number of culverts and cattle guards and nearly 35 miles of track."

Despite all the destruction and the agony exerted to achieve it, trains were again running from Louisville to Nashville by February 1.

7

THE BIG RAID

NEWS OF THE Battle of Stone's River dampened whatever elation Morgan might have felt about the success of his Christmas Raid in Kentucky. Although the damage he did to the Federal supply line was great, he realized that it had not come soon enough.

On December 26, just as Morgan was beginning to make a shambles of the railroad in Kentucky, Rosecrans had marched from Nashville toward Murfreesboro to challenge Bragg's Confederate army. Needless to say, Mattie Morgan's ball scheduled for that night was hastily canceled, and the entire city battened down the hatches to prepare for the invasion.

Some historians have recorded the battle as a tactical victory for Bragg and a strategic victory for Rosecrans. When it was over, Bragg had retreated to Tullahoma, and Rosecrans occupied Bragg's old stand at Murfreesboro. History records, too, that with Stone's River added to the defeat at Fort Donelson and the "probable loss" at Shiloh, the Confederacy had lost what amounted to three major battles in Tennessee, none of which it could afford.

After the Stone's River battle, General Joseph Wheeler, under whose command Bragg had placed both Morgan and Forrest, set up headquarters at McMinnville, forty miles east of Murfreesboro. There Morgan was reunited with his wife.

The nagging winter that had plagued Morgan in Kentucky continued unabated; and shortages of equipment, shelter, and sometimes food made things even more difficult. The Raiders kept active despite the weather, but on many occasions Morgan was not with them. It was general knowledge throughout Bragg's command that Morgan was spending more and more time with his bride and was paying less and less attention to his military duties. Some went so far as to say that never again would he be the daring raider that he once had been. One of Morgan's uncles became worried about the general becoming such a homebody and wrote in a letter to Mattie: "Now you must not get angry with me for saying to you I feel that you are sticking too close to your husband."

Mattie Morgan was blissfully happy even under the hardships of living in an army camp while Federals were enjoying the comforts of her father's home at Murfreesboro. Enviously her sister Alice wrote from Nashville: "You think the honeymoon will never end, don't you!"

Mattie wrote back:

"My life is one joyous dream now, from which I fear to awaken. . . . I can correspond almost regularly with you now, Sis. The bearer goes principally on my account."

What Mattie did not know was that the man who so willingly carried her letters back and forth between McMinnville and Nashville was a Yankee spy.

She continued to write:

"I know my liege-lord is devoted to me, and each day I am forced to love him more. . . . I have made me an elegant evening dress, a beautiful rose deschaune color, with a black lace flounce around the bottom, a black lace vest and sleeves, and a fall of black lace around the waist. . . . it is magnificent."

Only a few more letters were exchanged before a number of people were rounded up by the spy network and sent to jail—among them, Mattie's sister.

Under conditions such as these, citations did not mean a great deal to Morgan, but for what it was worth, he received from the Confederate Congress at Richmond a joint resolution commending him for his raid into Kentucky. "*Resolved by the Congress of the Confederate States of America:* That the thanks of Congress are due, and are hereby tendered to Gen. John H. Morgan, and the officers and men of his command, for their varied, heroic, and invaluable services in Tennessee and Kentucky, immediately preceding the battle before Murfreesboro—services which have conferred upon their authors fame as enduring as the records of the struggle which they have so brilliantly illustrated. Approved May 17, 1863."

Even the coming of another spring in Tennessee was not enough to lift the morale of Confederate troops stationed at McMinnville and Tullahoma. Morgan looked about but was not pleased with what he saw. After a most trying winter the army seemed to be coming apart at the seams; there were still shortages, even though the supply line was open all the way to Atlanta. There was a scarcity of horses, for one thing, and without them Morgan knew he could not operate. In addition many of his old Green River stalwarts were gone, among them St. Leger Grenfell, who had left before the Christmas Raid. Some whose services he had valued highly and upon whom he had constantly depended had lost their lives during the past several months. Even Basil Duke, injured while attempting to cross Rolling Fork River en route to Bardstown in December, was now recuperating in Georgia and unavailable to Morgan.

Duke would come back, but Morgan, who always relied on his brother-in-law more than anyone ever knew, realized that he needed more. His command was deteriorating, too. The men had become so careless that they had failed to detect a group of Federals who slipped through his lines and nearly brought disaster.

Henry Campbell, a sixteen-year-old boy from Crawfordsville, Indiana, serving with the Eighteenth Indiana Artillery Battery at Murfreesboro, recorded this event in his diary: "Reville this a.m. at 3 o'clock. Moved at 4, infantry taking the direct road to McMinnville our destination . . . captured the picket post and then, without loss of time . . . led a saber charge through town. John Morgan's force scattered in every direction. . . . The scouts came very near capturing Morgan himself; he escaped by the fleetness of his horse. . . . Seen General Morgan's wife while riding through town."

As it turned out, the general and Mattie had both managed to escape, though by different routes. Mattie was captured briefly on the road to Sparta, but when the Federal officer in charge discovered who she was, he gallantly set her free to continue her journey.

After that needless crisis, Morgan became impatient and felt that he needed another raid, something spectacular to give the Confederate morale a boost and at the same time pump some enthusiasm into his men. The trifling activity during the winter and spring had been little more than routine, and the duties to which they had been assigned by Wheeler were far beneath their talents. In Morgan's estimation, he and his Raiders were simply wasting their time.

Morgan cast about for possibilities, but his most exciting idea was practically dropped into his lap. That spring a Federal colonel and a detachment of Union cavalry had made a raid all the way through Mississippi and Louisiana to Baton Rouge. After learning of that raid, Morgan approached Bragg with the idea of a similar raid in the states north of the Ohio River. On the way, he would hit Kentucky again, destroy what Federal supplies he found, and get in a few more telling blows at his favorite whipping boy, the L & N Railroad.

The Kentucky raid would be fine, Bragg agreed, but

as for crossing the Ohio River, his answer was No. All Bragg needed, he said, was for Morgan to make a threat against Louisville; such a diversionary raid was all that would be necessary. If the city ran true to form, just a threat would cause panic in the streets, thundering editorials by George Prentice, and dozens of telegraph messages to Washington by the general in charge. That would be enough to ease pressure on his Army of Tennessee. Meanwhile, Bragg could move behind the Tennessee River at Chattanooga.

In the latter part of May 1863 Morgan ordered his command to concentrate in the area between Liberty and Alexandria, Tennessee. Supplies began to arrive in volume from Chattanooga, and horses by the hundreds were driven in from eastern Kentucky. Within a few days Morgan's division totaled almost 3,000 men, all completely outfitted and eager to march.

On June 10 Morgan rode into Alexandria as only he could ride—"a most imposing figure in the saddle," is the way Basil Duke described him. Today he was dressed in a brand new uniform, complete with all the gold braid that went with his rank of general. No mistake about it—John Hunt Morgan was the finest figure of a man one would be likely to see during the war.

Officers of his command crowded into regimental headquarters that evening for the news, and it was not long in coming. Morgan told them he had orders from General Bragg to make another raid in Kentucky, possibly as far as Louisville. Then, he said, if the situation warranted, he would cross the Ohio River into Indiana and perhaps head for Ohio.

Morgan told only Basil Duke that Bragg had not given him permission to cross the Ohio. Duke said later that he was not present when Bragg and Morgan discussed the proposed river crossing, but "General Morgan told me," Duke went on, "that General Bragg had ordered him to operate [only] in Kentucky, and further stated that he intended, notwithstanding [Bragg's] orders, to cross the Ohio."

Apparently Morgan had made his plans for the river crossing even before he and Bragg had completed their discussions about it, for he had ordered Duke three weeks earlier to send a scouting party to points along the Ohio River to find the best place for the Raiders to cross. Even then, Tom Hines, who had done a great deal of Morgan's scouting and intelligence work, was across the Ohio in Indiana.

Morgan's regiment crossed the Cumberland River on July 2, flooded though it was, and on the fourth tangled with the Federals at Tebb's Bend at a bridge near Campbellsville. After a fruitless and frustrating three-hour battle, Morgan called off the attack and bypassed the bridge, but the stop was costly. He left 71 dead or wounded, and Major James McCreary noted in his diary: "The commencement of this raid is ominous."

As Morgan progressed across Kentucky, newspapers, particularly those at Louisville, spread the word:

> MORGAN HAS 4,000 MEN; WILL STRIKE FRANKFORT
> MORGAN HAS 7,500 MEN; TARGET—CINCINNATI
> LOUISVILLE OBJECTIVE OF MORGAN'S 11,000 MEN

Such news would have delighted Morgan had he been reading those newspapers. Instead, he was meeting considerable resistance at Lebanon, and during that rather bloody battle his brother Tom took a Federal bullet through the chest and died in his brother Calvin's arms.

From Lebanon, Morgan headed for his predetermined target—the Ohio River. The attempted crossing would be forty miles west of Louisville at Brandenburg, the seat of Meade County, opposite Maukport, Indiana. When the general arrived, his advance detachment had done its work well. Tied up at the foot of Brandenburg's

Main Street were two steamboats, the *J. T. McCombs* and the *Alice Dean.* Morgan's ferry to Indiana was ready.

A small steamer, the *Lady Pike,* which had been converted to service as a gunboat, hove to; and when the captain saw what was going on, he raced away to Leavenworth, Indiana, eighteen miles downstream, and spread the word: "Morgan is at Brandenburg and will invade Indiana tomorrow!"

As the first troops of Morgan's command boarded the boats, a detachment of Harrison County, Indiana, Home Guards set up an ancient cannon mounted on the chassis of a farm wagon on the north side of the river. One round from the Raiders' artillery, located on the high bluff west of Brandenburg, scattered the Indiana defenders, and the river crossing proceeded without further ado. By midnight the job was complete. A torch was set to the *Alice Dean.* She burned to the water line and the smoldering hull sank in the muddy waters of the river. The *McCombs,* however, escaped destruction, thanks to Basil Duke's long friendship with her captain. Upon her release, the *McCombs* hurried away to Louisville, where the captain reported that by actual count 4,800 men, 5,000 horses, two six-pounder cannon, and two twelve-pounders had been transported from Kentucky to Indiana that night. The invasion of Yankeeland was under way.

The Raiders found Indiana to be a land of milk and honey. The countryside to which they had been accustomed had been foraged time and time again, but here were farms untouched by war; where families fled before the Raiders arrived, the food and supplies were there for the taking.

As the word spread, every municipality in Indiana expected Morgan to show up. When darkness closed in, the entire southern part of the state was frantically trying to do something to defend property and lives. The next day at Corydon the Raiders met their first resistance. There were 400 Home Guards barricaded in the former Indiana capital, but only a few minutes were required for Morgan's seasoned troopers to subdue them. It was at Corydon that Morgan learned General Robert E. Lee had been turned back during the Battle of Gettysburg. This was a blow for Morgan, because he had secretly hoped to join General Lee in Pennsylvania, if things went well for them both. In spite of the news, Morgan knew there was no turning back now.

At Indianapolis the governor of Indiana declared a state of emergency and pleaded with General Boyle at Louisville to "return some of our troops so we can make an adequate defense of our state." Meanwhile, notices were posted throughout the city: "In order to provide against possible danger it is requested that all . . . able bodied white male citizens will form themselves into companies and arm themselves with such arms as they can procure."

More than 60,000 men from all parts of Indiana responded as newspapers reported Morgan marching with 8,000 men toward the area of New Albany and Jeffersonville "where tremendous government stores are located."

Terror continued to spread through the state, and after a few hours of rest Morgan moved his command out of Corydon the afternoon of July 9. With strong detachments on both flanks, his men swept across a wide area as they headed toward Salem. En route, they hit Greenville, Palmyra, and Paoli, looting at each place. A large bridge on the New Albany & Salem Railroad proved to be too tempting—after all, railroad bridges were their speciality. They stopped to set a torch to it and tore up track for some distance on each side. Many years later that line would become a part of Morgan's old railroad foe, the L & N.

At Salem, Morgan toyed with the idea of heading toward Indianapolis and making good his threat of releasing the 6,000 Confederate prisoners confined there. An arsenal and huge stocks of military supplies located nearby would have enabled him to equip each prisoner adequately for a march back to Kentucky. Had he driven north with the speed he usually mustered during his raids, many strategists feel that he could well have made good his threat. Indianapolis lay practically undefended, but Morgan was unaware of that and turned eastward toward the state of Ohio.

The Federals were not far behind him. Anticipating Morgan's raid into Kentucky—but certainly not expecting the Ohio crossing—General James M. Shackleford had moved his command east from Russellville, Kentucky, in Logan County, to head him off. General Hobson had told Shackleford he thought Morgan would enter Kentucky at Burkesville and head for Columbia; as it turned out he was right, but when General H. M. Judah moved part of Hobson's command from Columbia to Glasgow, he created an unguarded gap through which the Raiders quickly passed. Then the Federals began the long chase.

The *Alice Dean* was still burning when General Hobson arrived at Brandenburg a few hours after Morgan had completed his crossing of the Ohio River. In a report written later, General Shackleford said: "When we came within two miles of Brandenburg, we discovered smoke rising from the burning transport that had set the enemy across the river, and heard shouts of triumph. We were 24 hours in attaining transports and crossing the river."

Once across, Hobson's men quickly picked up Morgan's trail along the rural Indiana roads. When they reached Corydon, they were only twenty-five miles behind Morgan, and the trail was becoming easier to follow, mainly because of the increased looting by the men.

Basil Duke made no attempt to gloss over the pillaging in his account of the raid:

This disposition for wholesale plunder exceeded anything that any of us had ever seen before. The men seemed actuated by a desire to "pay off" in the "enemy country" all the scores that the Federal army had chalked up in the South.

Each man who could get one, tied a bolt of calico to his saddle and let it unwind, only to throw it away and get a fresh one at the first opportunity. . . . One man carried a bird cage with three canaries in it for two days, and another rode with a chafing dish on the pummel of his saddle until an officer made him throw it away. . . . I could not believe that such a passion could have developed . . . among any body of civilized men.

From Salem the Raiders headed through Canton, New Philadelphia, and Vienna, where they burned the railroad depot and a nearby bridge, destroying several yards of track. They continued toward Lexington, eight miles farther, where they set up camp for the night.

The next morning they headed toward Vernon and North Vernon and about midnight stopped near Dupont. As it happened, a wealthy meat packer in Dupont had 2,000 prime hams in storage and needless to say, many of the troopers had a whole ham to add to their plunder. The packer's daughter gave the group a piece of her mind about their wanton stealing. After she had finished, one of Morgan's men commented on her beauty and predicted: "After we git through lickin' you Yankees, I'm gonna come back up here and marry you." As the story goes, he did come back and make good his promise. Many of the couple's descendants still live in the area.

Morgan found the heavily wooded Indiana hills much to his liking. The terrain was perfect for a continuing series of hit-and-run raids, but on this trip he did not have the time. On July 12 he rode into Versailles and captured 300 militia, one of the easiest exploits of the entire Indiana expedition. It was at Versailles, though, that the men resorted to outright thievery. Five thousand dollars disappeared from the county treasury, and one light-fingered Raider even made off with the coin-silver jewelry of the local Masonic lodge. When word of that deed reached Morgan, a Mason himself, he ordered the jewelry returned and the man court-martialed.

Still trailing Morgan, Hobson stubbornly held on in his pursuit; but he was able to capture only those completely exhausted from the constant travel, who stopped for a few hours of sleep and awoke as prisoners. As the Raiders moved on, their plight became more precarious. With an average of eighteen hours a day in the saddle for many days now, they were resorting to a trick they had learned a long time ago, sleeping in the saddle while still moving forward.

Monday afternoon they crossed the Ohio state line at Harrison. Morgan passed through Glendale, just north of Cincinnati, that night, and at daybreak, the Raiders rested in sight of the pickets around a Federal army camp. Then, just to keep things lively, they burned a wagon train, skirmished with a group of Federals, and galloped off toward open country with a couple of dozen excellent horses found in a nearby stable.

The general was at Williamsburg by midafternoon, twenty-eight miles east of Cincinnati. Just beyond Batavia, Morgan divided his forces and sent his brother Richard south to Georgetown while he himself continued eastward, passing through Mount Orab, Sardinia, and Winchester. Meanwhile, Richard had hit Ripley and West Union. Their two forces were reunited at Locust Grove on July 15.

As the Raiders passed through these Ohio communities, the pillaging and looting sometimes were worse than they had been in Indiana. At each town they touched, the populace watched in terror as the Raiders stole horses, broke into stores and helped themselves to the merchandise, tore up railroad tracks, and burned down depots. At Chillicothe, when word was received that Morgan was on the way, the defenders rushed out to the river and burned the bridge themselves. Meanwhile, many people threw their cherished household silver into wells and cisterns, and many a horse was hustled away to be hidden in the woods until the Raiders had gone.

On July 16 Morgan arrived at the banks of the Scioto River, where the Raiders paused and looted the towns of Jasper and Piketon. The next day, after riding forty-five miles, they looted Jackson and then dashed on to Vinton, where they bedded down for the night.

By now it was apparent that Morgan was heading for Buffington Ford at Portland, a small steamboat landing on the north bank of the Ohio opposite Buffington Island. There, the Raiders could ford the river and escape into West Virginia. With the river so close, Morgan's luck seemed to be running out. When he reached Portland, he found a detachment of Federals waiting. His educated guess was that about 300 men were between him and the river, and so rather than risk a night attack, Morgan decided to wait until daylight. Oddly enough, when dawn came, the earthworks behind which the Federals had been waiting had been abandoned and Morgan had an open road to the river. But the columns had scarcely gotten in motion when Hobson's forces, now joined by those of Major General Judah, finally caught up and attacked the Raiders from the rear. Simultaneously, two gunboats began shelling Morgan's position from the river. Basil Duke took a stand along the Pomeroy Road and was making a respectable show of resistance, but the attack was overwhelming. Tired from over two weeks of constant riding, Morgan's men went down in face of a superior force of Federals. The Raiders suffered 120 casualties and 700 were captured, including Duke and Richard Morgan. By his brave but losing stand, Duke had accomplished one thing: he had delayed the Federals just long enough for Morgan and nearly 1,200 of the men to escape Hobson's trap.

Seeking to take advantage of the very precious time that Duke had bought, Morgan and the remainder of the

Raiders galloped away toward Reidsville, fifteen miles upstream from Buffington Island, where they made another attempt to cross the river. About 300 of the men made it across before the two gunboats showed up. Morgan, halfway across astride his horse Glencoe, turned back rather than leave the majority of his men stranded in Ohio without leadership.

Morgan's time had not yet run out. From here, he began a running fight that was to last another week. With fewer than 900 men now, the general circled back to Vinton County, and on the night of the twentieth he camped at Valley Furnace. They met the enemy that day at Hockingport, Coal Hill, and Cheshire; then for a day and a night they rode without stopping, passing through Eagle Furnace and Vinton Station. By one o'clock in the morning of July 22, Morgan and his 900 bedraggled refugees were at Zaleski, and later were seen passing through Mount Pleasant and New Plymouth. The sweltering heat, which had plagued them since they landed in Indiana, began to take its toll, and beyond Nelsonville and New Straitsville men began to straggle behind. At a point south of Taylorsville, on the Muskingum River, horses were falling from heat exhaustion and men dropped off to sleep and tumbled from their saddles.

At Eagleport a company of Federals, the Eighty-sixth Ohio Volunteer Infantry, waited for the Raiders to arrive; but they failed to consider that Morgan was still capable of the unexpected. He crossed the Muskingum there after dark, while the Federals slept, and managed to evade a company of militia near Blue Rock en route to Cumberland.

On the morning of July 24 the decrepit columns, traveling now with no effort at military order, were at Campbell Station, east of Cambridge. About midmorning they skirmished with militia at Old Washington and by nightfall they were at Hendrysburg.

Morgan, apparently still looking for an opportunity to

cross the Ohio River into West Virginia, headed east toward Harrisville. He skirmished again at New Athens, passed through Smithfield and Wintersville (not far from Steubenville), and clashed with militia again at Richmond. On the night of July 25, the Raiders were almost to the limit of their endurance. As they stopped at Bergholz, the men slid off their horses and fell asleep where they lay.

Pursuers caught up with them early Sunday, July 26, but they still had some fight left. Morgan fled north to Salineville, where at eight o'clock the Ninth Michigan Cavalry overtook him and the remnants of his command. The Federals could hardly believe what they saw. Morgan had formed a battle line, and during the brief encounter thirty of the Raiders were killed, about 50 wounded, and 200 taken prisoner. When it was over, Morgan and several hundred of the men had escaped. The chase continued.

The end came six hours later when Morgan surrendered, realizing that further flight was useless and cruel to the men who were still with him. The site was a field near West Point in Columbiana County on what is now State Route 518, approximately six miles south of Lisbon, scarcely more than sixty miles from Lake Erie. Incredibly, the raid had covered eleven hundred miles.

A telegram sent by Major George W. Rue of the Ninth Federal Kentucky Cavalry read: "I captured John Morgan today at two o'clock P.M., taking 336 prisoners, 400 horses and arms."

In 1909 Will I. Thompson of East Liverpool erected a stone monument near the surrender site on which is a plaque that bears these words: "This Stone Marks the Spot Where the Confederate Raider, Gen. John H. Morgan Surrendered His Command to Major Geo. W. Rue July 26, 1863, and is the Farthest Point North Ever Reached by Any Body of Confederate Troops During the Civil War."

8

FREEDOM'S WAY

VENGEANCE WAS SWIFT. Within days Morgan and most of his officers had been placed in temporary confinement at the Cincinnati jail. Ohio's Governor David Tod insisted that they were civil prisoners and should be treated as such; thus he ordered their transfer to the Ohio State Penitentiary at Columbus.

On July 30, with the weather still sweltering hot, Morgan and a number of his officers and men (eventually 68 in all) were transferred under heavy guard from Cincinnati to Columbus to prison. There they were stripped, scrubbed, and shaven of their hair, beards, and moustaches. When Basil Duke arrived a few days later to be confined at the same prison, he failed to recognize the shorn Morgan until he spoke.

The confinement was most galling to these men, who had been accustomed to an active outdoor life. Their boredom was eased somewhat by the use of a ladder as an exercise bar. Otherwise they whiled away their time at chess, cards, and reading; a few even played marbles. Duke wrote poems, and Morgan wrote many letters to his wife, expressing his love and devotion. He also wrote letters to government officials, protesting their being confined as ordinary criminals. On occasion the men managed to get a newspaper to read.

As the time passed, discipline became more strict,

and the men were placed in solitary confinement for even the slightest infraction of the rules, such as talking after the lights were out.

After nearly three months the men realized that they were not going to be paroled nor even permitted to have visitors (Morgan's mother had been turned away after making a trip from Lexington to Columbus). Thus their thoughts turned toward possibilities of escape. The odds were certainly not in their favor. In addition to the problem of the barred cells, the prison walls were made of heavy brick, and beyond them was an outer wall some twenty-five feet high.

At first, escape talk seemed ridiculous, and Morgan and the others laughed when twenty-five-year-old Tom Hines suggested that they might dig a tunnel. The fact that the prison had concrete floors made that idea sound all the more preposterous. Hines's idea turned out to be more feasible than they had thought. He had noticed that a portion of the concrete floor through the cells was always dry, although surrounding areas were often moist from condensation. A casual conversation with one of the older deputies one day verified the fact that an air duct was located below the cell block. When Hines told the others about this, they were indeed elated. Now all they needed was some implement to chip the concrete. Two table knives were secreted from the prison dining room, and the men went to work after the lights were out, chipping away at the concrete floor in Tom Hines's cell. The powdered concrete went into a stove in the hall; larger pieces were disposed of in Hines's mattress, which grew somewhat uncomfortable before the job was finished. As it turned out, the concrete was six inches thick, and it took them three days to chip away a hole about fourteen inches in diameter. Below that was a brick arch, six courses thick. The hole in the floor was kept covered by Hines's carpetbag, and since inspections were few and far between, the hole was not discovered until after the escape. Once the brick arch had been removed, the men wormed their way into the four-foot-square air duct and began their tunnel. The knives, now considerably worn, were replaced with a shovel they had managed to bring in from the coal pile in the prison yard. It had a broken handle, but it enabled them to work at a much greater speed.

There were other problems, of course. The tunnel would surface inside the prison yard where dogs were kept; and once in the yard, they would have to scale the twenty-five-foot wall. They decided to take care of the dogs when the time came. If it rained they would be confined in their kennels on the opposite side of the yard anyway. For scaling the wall they would need a rope, and Calvin Morgan, brother of the general, braided one thirty feet long from strips of their bedspreads. A hook made from an iron poker (taken from the stove in the hall) was attached to one end of Calvin's rope. At the proper time it would be tossed to the top of the wall, where, with luck, it would catch on the coping securely enough that they could climb the rope.

The tunnel was completed on November 20, and the men met that night to decide on a plan. It was understood from the beginning that Morgan would go first. If their plan was a success—the Raiders never discussed failures—the general would be free to reorganize his old command or to form a new one. It was also decided that no more than six men should accompany Morgan in this attempt.

The question of where to go after they had gotten outside the prison was basically one of whether they should head for Canada or go directly toward the Ohio River. The Canadian route was abandoned as being too risky. In addition, it would take Morgan too long to get back below Confederate lines. The more direct route, and the more obvious in case they should be found out, would also be dangerous. A day-old newspaper, secured from a guard, provided a railroad schedule that listed a train on the Little Miami Railroad as leaving Columbus for Cincinnati at one o'clock in the morning. The train departure set the time for their move. Since the guard inspected the cells at midnight, the attempt to escape would have to be a few minutes after the inspection was over, or whenever the guard had finished his job and returned to his post in another part of the building. They could not wait long, for Morgan had to have time to get to the railroad station before one o'clock in order to catch the train.

It is not known how the six men chosen to accompany Morgan were selected. Basil Duke recorded the list: Captains Thomas H. Hines, Ralph Sheldon, Sam B. Taylor (nephew of General Zachary Taylor), Jacob C. Bennett, James D. Hockersmith, and Gustavus S. McGee. Hines would go with Morgan to catch the train, and the others would scatter in different directions.

The night of November 27 was selected. At midnight the guard made his rounds. After he had gone, the seven men hastily but quietly knocked the concrete from the openings they had carved under their cells and moved into the air duct. Fortunately for their plans, it had begun to rain, and long before they broke the soil to open the tunnel into the prison yard, sentries had confined the dogs in their kennels and sought shelter themselves. The rope and hook worked perfectly; the rest was easy.

Morgan and Hines hurried to the railroad station. The next morning, when the train slowed briefly in the outskirts of Cincinnati, both men leaped off and quickly headed for the Ohio River. They spotted a boy in a skiff near the shore and, for two dollars, persuaded him to row them to the Kentucky side. When they landed at Ludlow, just below Covington, the time was about seven o'clock, certainly not too early to knock on the door of a friend's house. The friend invited them in for breakfast and later furnished them with horses. That day they rode twenty-eight miles to Union, in Boone County. Following a trail something like an underground railroad heading south, the two men traveled in easy stages, breathing easier with each mile they put between themselves and the Ohio River. On occasion they had volunteer guides to steer them around the many areas that were well populated by Federal army units. Onward they went through Gallatin, Owen, Henry, Shelby, Spencer, Nelson, LaRue, Green, Metcalf, and Cumberland counties in Kentucky. On December 8, they reached Livingston, Tennessee, and once more were on familiar ground.

Back in Ohio the news of Morgan's escape had spread quickly. By the morning of November 29, newspapers all over the country carried banner stories about it. Confederates cheered and clung a little tighter to their faint hope of one more big victory somewhere along the way. The Federals underwent a period of faultfinding. The army blamed Governor Tod for Morgan's escape, while the governor blamed the army; the controversy raged for weeks. Eventually, Governor Tod posted a $5,000 reward for Morgan's capture.

By Christmas, the general was reunited with Mattie in Columbia, South Carolina, where she had fled after Bragg's retreat to Chattanooga in July. She had found refuge at various times in Augusta, Georgia, Knoxville, Tennessee, and Danville, Virginia. It was at Danville where she had lost her expected child, so the report goes, after that long and arduous trip from Tennessee.

On April 7, 1865, Mattie's second child, a daughter, was born, but the general did not live to see her. Mattie named her Johnnie—Johnnie Hunt Morgan—in honor of her father. In 1883 Johnnie attended a reunion of Morgan's men in Lexington and was presented with a gold watch. She was married May 1, 1888 to Joseph W. Caldwell, a young Presbyterian minister of Selma, Alabama. The wedding, held in Lebanon, Tennessee, was a private and quiet affair with only a few friends present "on account of the recent death of the young lady's mother," stated the Lebanon *Herald.* Shortly after the wedding, Johnnie's husband was selected by his church to attend the Pan American Presbyterian Council meeting in London, England. After he sailed, Johnnie returned to Lebanon to visit maternal relatives and contracted typhoid fever. She died June 28 before her husband's ship arrived in England. They had been married less than two months. She was buried in Cedar Grove Cemetery in Lebanon, near the grave of her mother. Years later, Dr. Laben Lacy Rice, in his 100th year remembered Johnnie Morgan as "a refined lady, a real aristocrat."

Early in January 1864, General and Mrs. Morgan made a triumphal entry into Richmond, Virginia. The adulation poured upon the general and his wife by the friendly people was not offered them by the Confederate high command. Morgan was sure the official coldness was the fault of Bragg, now Davis's special military advisor, who was still miffed over the direct disobedience of his orders not to cross the Ohio River. Bragg also reminded Morgan that he had been away from Murfreesboro during the Battle of Stone's River on one of those infernal raids into Kentucky just when he was most needed.

Morgan took both the adulation and the criticism in stride. Numerous receptions in his honor were scheduled throughout the city. Those attending one special affair held at city hall included such Kentuckians as Provisional Governor Hawes and Generals Jeb Stuart and Ambrose P. Hill, one of Morgan's brothers-in-law. Another guest was Morgan's old comrade St. Leger Grenfell, who had walked away for good the day before the Raiders left on the Christmas Raid; Tom Hines, who had been captured in Tennessee but was now safe in Richmond, and Robert A. Alston, former *Vidette* editor, who had just been exchanged, also managed to attend.

Morgan spent most of January in Richmond attempting to secure authorization for a new command. Unfortunately he ran into a maze of red tape everywhere he turned. No doors were opened, and he was sure that General Bragg was behind much of his inability to see even a few of the right people. After failing to get an appointment with James Seddon, the Confederate Secretary of War, he wrote him a letter requesting permission to assemble a command in southwestern Virginia. His proposal included an invasion of Kentucky to bring back cavalry horses badly needed by the Confederacy. He explained to the secretary that reliable reports indicated at least 15,000 suitable horses in Kentucky, 5,000 in Lexington alone. A well-planned raid, such as he could carry out with a great degree of success, would not only enable them to acquire horses but would help relieve Yankee pressure at Chattanooga.

It was a good proposal, the secretary admitted, but Morgan got nowhere. With Bragg still hinting that he might court-martial Morgan for disobeying orders, the general and his wife left Richmond in disgust. In self-exile, Morgan spent February 1864 in Decatur, Georgia, attempting to reassemble the remnants of his old command, chiefly through a proclamation he had printed and circulated.

SOLDIERS: *I am once more among you, after a long and painful imprisonment. I am anxious to be again in the field. I therefore call on all the soldiers of my command to assemble at once at the rendezvous which has been established at this place. . . . Come at once, and come cheerfully, for I want no man in my command who has to be sent to his duty by a provost marshal. The work before us will be arduous, and will require brave hearts and willing hands. Let no man falter or delay, for no time is to be lost. Every one must bring his horse and gun who can.*

JOHN H. MORGAN
Brigadier General Provisional Army Confederate States.

Apparently Morgan's personal magnetism still worked. Men flocked into Decatur from throughout the South to help form a new command. They set up their own quartermaster corps, and from the ranks came blacksmiths, saddlemakers, and other artisans who could make or supply many of the items needed to equip a new military command. By early spring, many members of Morgan's old command had heard of or seen his proclamation and began to drift into Decatur.

It was inevitable that Morgan would feel that another trip to Richmond was in order. This time he won his argument with the Confederate bureaucrats and was assigned just what he wanted—the Department of Southwestern Virginia, with headquarters at Abingdon. He was given not only the cavalry units he had so painstakingly put together at Decatur but also a group of dismounted men then stationed at Dalton, Georgia.

In April orders were received at Decatur for the men to march to Virginia and join their commander. By May they were encamped at Saltville. The area was rather well blessed, what with the salt works, and, near Wytheville, a lead mine to assure them of an unending supply of bullets. The spring of 1864 now looked much more promising than the preceding one had. Much had happened in the twelve months in between, but Morgan was not one to look back. By the middle of May, the general's brigade had increased to about 2,000 men, and he had horses enough for about two-thirds of them.

Near the end of May, Morgan began to concentrate his forces near Wytheville, and on the thirty-first he fired off a message to the Confederate War Department at Richmond, not asking them but *telling* them that he was starting on a raid into Kentucky to bring back horses. As a sort of postscript he added: "There is nothing in the State to retard my progress but a few scattered provost guards."

Long before the message arrived at Richmond, the columns had left Virginia and entered Letcher County, Kentucky through Pound Gap. John Morgan was on his last raid in Kentucky.

9

LAST LOOK AT KENTUCKY

AN UNEASY PEACE in Kentucky, one that had lasted almost a year, was broken on the morning of June 8, 1864, at Cynthiana.

On that particular morning, the quiet, sun-drenched stillness was interrupted as two men on horseback galloped down the town's main street like self-appointed Paul Reveres. "Morgan! Morgan! Listen everybody! John Hunt Morgan is headed this way," they cried repeatedly as people who had been going about their morning chores stopped in shocked surprise.

Cynthiana residents well remembered the time nearly two years before when General Morgan and his men had laid seige to the city, and the effects of that battle at the covered bridge across the Licking River were still evident.

Word spread through the city as rapidly as "fire in a dry broomsedge field on a windy day," one report said, as residents paused, many with mixed emotions, wondering whether they were ready for or could survive another visit from John Hunt Morgan. Officially, or as officially as rumor-haunted reports would permit, Morgan and 2,000 men, had crossed into Kentucky six days ago, captured Owingsville, and then headed for Mount Sterling.

It was to be three days before an apprehensive population at Cynthiana would experience real war for the second time; meanwhile, Morgan's Raiders had indeed struck Mount Sterling that very day.

Morgan's columns had reached the vicinity of the Montgomery County seat early in the morning, and the general made preparations for an immediate attack on the Federals stationed there. During a dramatic charge shortly after daybreak, the surprised garrison of some 300 men was quickly overpowered. Reports of this action also say that the men began a systematic looting of the town. When the excitement had died down, most of the stores and some of the homes had been pillaged and the till of the Farmer's Bank of Kentucky was short, some say, $72,000. Blame for the bank robbery was ultimately placed on the regimental surgeon, Dr. R. R. Goode, who had disappeared in the confusion following the battle. Despite considerable investigation later, no one ever knew what happened to the surgeon or the missing $72,000.

From the ravaged main street of Mount Sterling, Morgan and the greater portion of his command headed toward Lexington, thirty-five miles away, where his intelligence reports indicated that the Union army had 5,000 horses quartered. The opportunity to be back home again in the Bluegrass was not lost upon the Kentuckians of Morgan's command. It was a clear, sunny day, and the countryside had never looked more beautiful, particularly to those who were coming home to it after so long. Thus the ride along the road toward Fayette County was one filled with laughter, jests, and good-natured bantering among the men—all this despite the fact that they had traveled over 250 miles during the past twelve days, much of it over mountainous country, with very little rest.

Morgan's scouts had done their work well, and when the general and his Raiders rode quietly into Lexington at 2 A.M. on June 10, they were able to make their way without opposition to their selected targets. The principal ones were several large warehouses scattered throughout the city, crammed with Federal supplies. Simultaneously, each structure, along with the railroad depot, was set afire. Within minutes smoke was rolling into the night sky and a flame-reddened pall quickly spread over the city. Soon the volunteer fire department was rushing to its task, and Morgan, a former member, must have been pleased with the way it responded to his night's work.

As the fires continued to rage, many of them out of control, squads of Raiders began to round up all the horses they could find, including several from the estate of Henry Clay. "Reliable rumors" to the contrary, when Morgan made a hasty count, his men had located only about 1,000 of the 5,000 horses reported to be quartered there. Sometime during the raid on Lexington the sum of $10,000 in cash disappeared from the Branch Bank of Kentucky.

The fires were still burning brightly when Morgan ordered his Raiders to take the horses and make for Paris. After the general watched the last man head down the Paris Pike, he whirled his horse and galloped toward Hopemont, where despite the early hour he would visit his mother. On the way one of the Federal patrols seems to have spotted the lone rider and given chase. As the story goes, one that by now is a Kentucky legend, when the Federals reached the corner where the old house stood, the horse and rider were nowhere to be seen. The patrol fanned out in the area for some distance around the Hunt home, but found nothing. Thinking that whoever they had been chasing had eluded them, they returned to camp.

Morgan had indeed eluded the Federals. As they galloped along not far behind him up Mill Street, he arrived at Hopemont and quickly rode his horse through the big double front doors, which were quickly closed and barred behind him. A servant held and calmed the

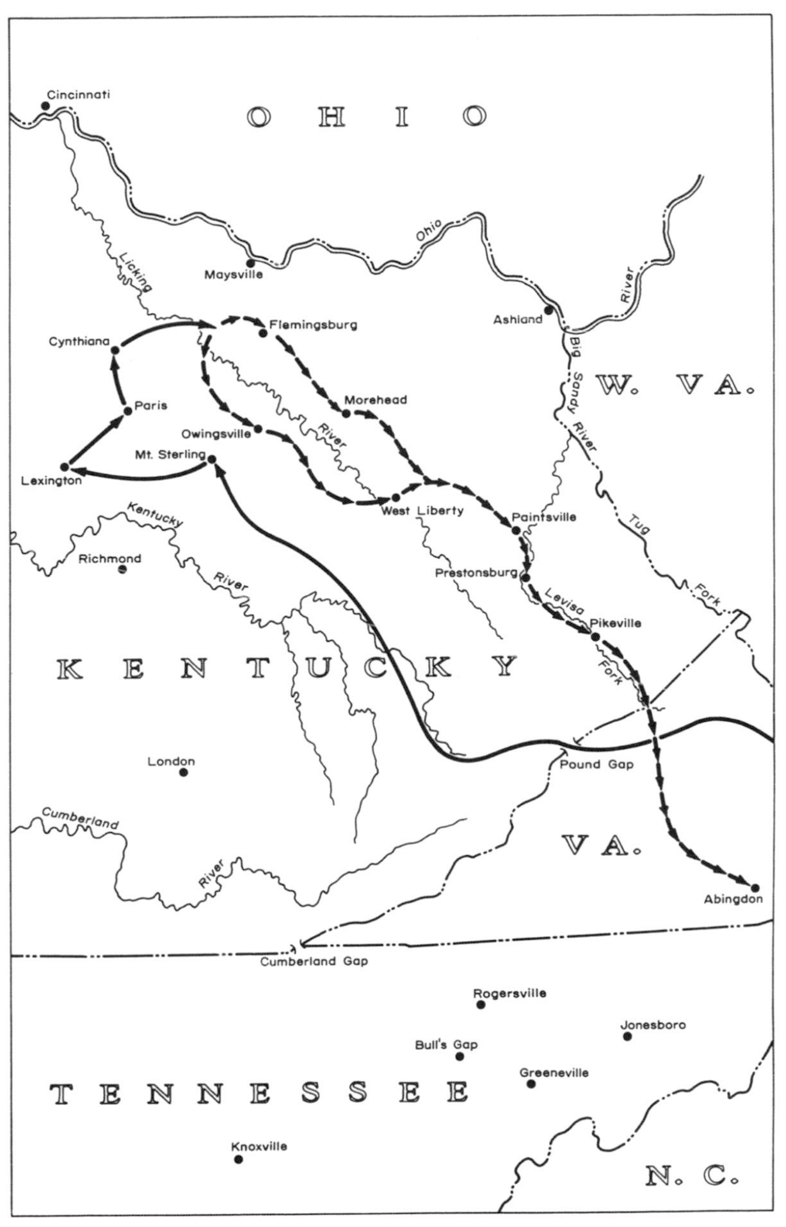

The Last Raid, June 1864

general's steed while he paid his respects to his mother. As soon as he was sure the Federals were gone, he led his horse out the back door. Before he rode away toward Paris, he looked back briefly at the home silhouetted against the glow of the firelit night sky. It was the last time he would see Hopemont.

Logically, with 1,000 horses to help supply the needs of the Confederacy, Morgan should have headed for Virginia. Instead, a few hours later, he and the Raiders had stopped at Paris for food and rest. While this brief stop was being made, Morgan's scouts were moving toward Cynthiana, fifteen miles away.

Earlier that morning when the "down train" from Covington arrived at Cynthiana on the Kentucky Central Railroad, the conductor was informed that Rebels were in the area to the south. Eager to keep his train out of danger, the conductor had the crew detach the locomotive from the passenger cars, couple it to a flatcar loaded with riflemen, and proceed quickly toward Paris. At Lair Station, three miles down the line, two Federal soldiers stood beside the track waving frantically.

"Morgan's men are coming!" they shouted and pointed toward Paris. The soldiers had been guarding the Townsend Creek bridge and explained to the conductor that Morgan's advance party had attacked them and blown up the trestle, setting fire to what was left. The guards had barely escaped and as they scrambled aboard the flatcar, the engineer threw the locomotive in reverse and began the return trip to Cynthiana. As the fearful news of Morgan's approach spread through Cynthiana for the second time in three days, the population was frantic. While the train crew began the task of replenishing supplies of wood and water for the locomotive, several hundred refugees with their belongings began to push their way aboard the railroad passenger cars. Among those climbing aboard were officials of the local bank, carrying bags bulging with currency and securities. With the word of the Mount Sterling raid fresh in their minds, they certainly did not want to take any risks when Morgan reached Cynthiana. The train pulled away toward Covington, leaving Cynthiana practically deserted. Those remaining were a small number of Confederate sympathizers and a Federal garrison of only a few hundred men.

The next day, true to their old habits, Morgan and his Raiders appeared at Cynthiana at daybreak. In contrast to the struggle two years before, this battle was an easy one. After a charge across a wheat field just outside of town, Morgan's men executed a slight flanking movement; a sharp skirmish in the center of town followed, and that was about the end of it. As a result of that skirmish, however, a fire broke out in a livery stable and spread rapidly through much of the business area, destroying several commercial buildings along with about twenty-five residences before it could be brought under control.

As the flames died down, Morgan and his officers gathered the citizens together and apologized for the inconvenience they had caused. That ceremony was halted abruptly as a scout rushed up to Morgan with the report that Federal troops were approaching from the north. The ability to make quick decisions was among Morgan's most valued talents, and he made a quick one at that time.

Reassembling his forces, Morgan prepared to meet the Federals—a detachment, he found out later, led by General Edward Hobson, the same officer who had pursued him across Ohio the year before. Hobson's Federals roared into Cynthiana, and there was another brisk encounter, this one including one of Morgan's famous mounted charges. One of the Federal soldiers later described it as being rather disconcerting because "they were yelling that infernal Rebel yell." After it was over, the Federals, nearly 1,000 of them, surrendered.

Morgan savored every moment of this surrender, and as he approached Hobson, he smiled graciously. "General, we meet again!" he is reported to have said, as Hobson handed over his pistols.

Burdened with 1,000 horses and 1,000 Federal prisoners, Morgan was faced with another decision. He had to leave Cynthiana, the horses he must take with him, but what was he to do with the prisoners? Several members of his command favored paroling them all, including General Hobson, and leaving immediately for Virginia. But Morgan, still enjoying the victory over his old adversary, decided to spend the night at Cynthiana and make his decision the next morning.

For once, Morgan did not leave orders to be ready for departure at daybreak. Instead, he permitted his command to sleep late and enjoy a leisurely breakfast. The sun had scarcely risen above the horizon when a shout of warning was heard throughout the camp. Within seconds General Stephen Burbridge, in command of a Federal force that outnumbered Morgan's two to one, rushed in with a long, crescent-shaped battle line and through sheer power began sweeping the Raiders in front of it. Many were trapped while still eating breakfast, and others were overpowered before they could reach their horses.

Hard hit, the Raiders fell back to the Licking River, where once more the covered bridge was the scene of panic. But this time it was the Rebels who were in trouble. The battle raged for several hours. Morgan had faced overwhelming odds before and somehow he had almost always been successful in overpowering or escaping the enemy. He and the Raiders fought stubbornly, but the outcome was never in doubt. Miraculously, over half of the Raiders escaped, including Morgan, but they were so badly scattered that it was several weeks before they found their several ways back to Virginia.

The retreat took Morgan, along with a small group of his Raiders, back across Kentucky through Flemingsburg, Morehead, West Liberty, Paintsville, Prestonsburg, and Pikeville. On June 20, they limped into Abingdon, Virginia, bone tired and heartsick. Even Morgan admitted that the raid was a complete failure; he had not been able to bring a single extra horse out of Kentucky.

10

A DAY OF DESTINY

IT WAS AUGUST before all the Raiders who had escaped Burbridge's troops returned to the rolling hills of southwestern Virginia. In the midst of that colorful summer landscape they paused to heal the wounds of battle. Every man seemingly moved back into his old place, and on the face of things, the indomitable spirit of the Raiders was as it always had been.

Mattie Morgan, who had been in South Carolina during the Cynthiana raid, rejoined the general, and her presence served to bolster his sagging spirits. As the command settled down to routine camp life, Mattie accompanied her husband on various inspection tours. Her sunny disposition helped to smooth some of the dissension that lay beneath the brave facade of the officers and men in her husband's command.

But the problem could not be solved by charm alone. Morgan faced the facts; there was no point in trying to evade the issue any longer. In spite of his daring and his nonchalance, he was a sensitive man, and his last Kentucky raid had been more than a failure; for him personally it had been a disaster. Censured severely for the Mount Sterling bank robbery and the burning and looting in Lexington and Cynthiana, Morgan lost much of the support of his civilian friends in Kentucky. Some types of criticism he could take. He had received censure before because war was war, people suffered, cities were burned. But if he had not made those raids, someone else would have. The censure from his own men because of the Mount Sterling robbery was a much sorer point.

Members of the old Second Kentucky had stood by him just as they always had since those Green River days, but somewhere along the line the comradeship of the command as a whole had changed. New men who had no feeling of loyalty or belonging—*really* belonging—had become part of the command, and it no longer was the same. Lieutenant Colonel Cally Alston had summed it up rather well earlier when he said: "These outrages are very disgraceful and are usually perpetrated by men accompanying the army for plunder. They are not worth a damn and are a disgrace to both armies."

Such thoughts troubled Morgan. During those trying days, John Castleman wrote of the general, "Low spirited, embarrassed by misfortune, he had not the buoyancy, nor the self-reliance which was his wont, and had not any longer his accustomed faculty of inspiring enthusiasm."

Eventually the criticism and censure that had at first been whispered throughout the camp had come out into the open. Apparently several of his officers, hoping to curry favor with Richmond, went over the general's head to report what they knew about the robbery at Mount Sterling.

After weighing the information he had—mostly unofficial reports and rumors—Secretary Seddon announced that a commission would be appointed to convene at Abingdon on September 10 for the purpose of investigating the accusations. That body would also look into the charge that Morgan had undertaken the ill-fated raid into Kentucky without orders. At the same time, Secretary Seddon announced that Brigadier General John C.

Echols would succeed Morgan in southwestern Virginia.

Before Echols could go to Abingdon, however, scouts reported to Morgan that a Federal force was headed for Bull's Gap, Tennessee, about ninety miles to the southwest. Since Echols had not arrived when Morgan received that news, he did what any other commanding officer would have done under similar circumstances—ordered the command to march. The army headed for Jonesboro, Tennessee, but, always the gentleman, Morgan said he would wait in Abingdon for his replacement to arrive.

Echols did not arrive, but Basil Duke did. He had been released from the Ohio prison and exchanged at Charleston, South Carolina. He wanted to join the expedition, but Morgan insisted that he use this opportunity to visit his wife, Henrietta, since she was at Abingdon and Duke had not seen her in many months. The brothers-in-law had a chance to talk for a while too, mostly discussing their prison life, the escape, and Duke's exchange. Duke walked with Morgan to the train on the Virginia & Tennessee Railroad that would take him to Jonesboro where he would join his command. Any other words that might have been exchanged between the two officers who had been through so much of the war together would never be said, for it was the last time Duke ever saw Morgan.

Speaking later of that last meeting, Duke said he was appalled at the general's appearance. "He was greatly changed, his face wore a weary, careworn expression, and his manner was totally destitute of its former ardor and enthusiasm. He spoke bitterly, but without impatience, of the clamor against him, and seemed saddest about the condition of his command. He declared that if he had been successful in the last day's fight at Cynthiana, he would have been enabled to hold Kentucky for months."

clinations. It is, with all due respect, that I express my regret that his application was successful.

Permit me again, sir, to urge earnestly, that the investigation, which can alone remove the difficulties which I now experience, shall be immediately ordered.

I have the honor to be, very respectfully,

Your obedient servant,

JOHN H. MORGAN.

To HON. JAMES A. SEDDON, Secretary of War.

As things turned out, it did not matter, but from all indications Morgan's letter was never sent to Secretary Seddons.

Morgan reached Jonesboro on September 1 and joined his command of approximately 1,600 men on the afternoon of the second. By midafternoon of the next day they had reached Greeneville. Scouting reports indicated that no enemy could be found anywhere in the area, and Morgan issued orders for the men to pitch camp.

As the Raiders began to dismount, Morgan noticed several large cumulus clouds that had rolled up in the sky behind the Smokies, and it looked as if there might be rain before morning. Morgan began making assignments of his forces for the night. One battery was placed atop a hill overlooking the town, and detachments were set up on roads leading to Bull's Gap and Rogersville and at the fork of the Newport and Warrensburg roads. As best he could judge from the map, the general had established protection on every major road leading into the city.

Morgan and his staff set up headquarters in the home of Mrs. Catherine Williams, who, some say, was an old friend of Morgan's. She was said to be a Confederate sympathizer, but since two of her sons were with the Confederate army and one with the Federals, certainly her loyalties were divided. It is known that her home had been visited a number of times by both Confederates and Federals when they were in the vicinity. The Williams residence was the largest in Greeneville, and the property covered an entire block. On the north side, occupying almost the whole area, was the large, substantial red brick house which fronted to the south. To the west and extending southward were stables and smaller outbuildings. Still further south, reaching to the opposite street, was a vineyard of considerable size. In the southeast corner of the property was a small frame church that stood on brick supports about three feet high. A profusion of trees, shrubs, and flowers made the lot one of the most attractive residential sites in the city. Adjacent to the house was a boxwood hedge; a high wood fence surrounded the rest of the property.

Morgan and his staff officers—Major Charles Withers, Harry Clay, and C. W. Gassett—were assigned sleeping quarters on the second floor and advised that supper would be served at six o'clock.

There are numerous and conflicting accounts of what happened during the next twelve hours. Some say that after the general arrived that afternoon, Lucy, the wife of the Unionist son, left hurriedly in a buggy, supposedly to go to the Williams farm several miles out of town to obtain watermelons for the guests. Major Withers said that Morgan ordered some of his men to follow her "to assist her in bringing back the melons." The party returned, reporting that they had not found Lucy nor had she been to the farm.

In any event, within an hour after she left, the rainstorm that had been brewing since the Raiders arrived that afternoon hit the Greeneville area, and pickets around the city scurried for shelter. Despite the rain, after Morgan and his staff had eaten supper they rode out to inspect the various outlying camps. At that time, all was well.

According to one of the staff officers, Morgan seemed restless that evening and several times before retiring checked to see if the sentries were on duty around the house as he had instructed them. What seemed to worry him was the still absent daughter-in-law, Lucy.

At daybreak Sunday morning a sentry roused Major Withers, who in turn walked across the hall and awakened the general. Morgan asked if it was still raining. Since it was, he suggested that the men be given time to dry their guns, setting departure time at seven. The rain stopped while Withers waited for the couriers to return to headquarters indicating that the general's orders had been received, and it looked as if the storm was over. He thought how nice it would be to have a clear day for marching.

The major finished dressing, and as he stepped into the hall he heard a rumbling sound—not thunder this time, but more like rifle fire. Rifle fire it was, and it was coming closer.

In a letter written in 1871, Major Withers gave this account of what followed:

> Hastening to the General's room, I found that he had gone out, and on searching, found him in the garden . . . in the vicinity of the church, and we took refuge under it to consult. He directed me to go to the top of the house and see if there was an opening through which he could pass. . . . [I] found every street blocked with [Federal] cavalry, while lines of men were riding around next to the plank fence shooting in all directions through the grounds. I could also see squads of men at the terminus of each street on the outskirts of the village. Reporting these facts to the General, I urged him to go into the house and there surrender, as it was our only chance and growing momentarily less as the fire was growing heavy and at point blank range. He replied: "It is useless; they have sworn never to take me a prisoner."
>
> Hearing the church being forced open, we crossed over into the vineyard . . . by almost crawling and taking advantage of every bush. . . . [I] again urged him to go into the house. This he refused to do, and [he suggested] we separate. . . . In leaving, the General shook hands with me and remarked:
>
> "You will never see me again."

I had gone but a few steps when I heard him call out: "Don't shoot, I surrender!"

Stopping immediately, I looked around and upon the outside of the fence almost over the General, who had risen and was holding up his hands, sat a Yankee with gun presented, who replied:

"Surrender and be God damned—I know you"—and fired. . . . As soon as the shot was fired and the General had fallen, the Yankee commenced shouting: "I've killed the damned horse thief," and began tearing down the fence.

Events surrounding the death of Morgan are confused. The Federal soldier said to have done the shooting, Private Andrew Campbell, of the Thirteenth Tennessee Union Cavalry, part of the command of General Alvin C. Gillem, threw the general's body across his horse and took it to show his commanding officer. Basil Duke said: "[Morgan's] friends have always believed that he was murdered after his surrender; his slayers broke down the paling around the garden in which they killed him, dragged him through, and while he was tossing his arms in his dying agonies, threw him across a mule, and paraded his body about the town—shouting and screaming in savage exultation."

Others contend there is no proof that Campbell killed Morgan. His body, they say, was struck by bullets from several rifles. Duke said flatly, "He was shot through the heart." In any event, even if he did not fire the fatal shot, Private Campbell was commissioned a lieutenant later, presumably for the part he played in Morgan's death. Many historians are inclined to accept the letter written by Major Withers as the most accurate account of what happened in those last few minutes of General Morgan's life there in the Williams garden.

Another puzzling question down through the years has been how the Federals found out Morgan was in the Williams house. Few believe that Mrs. Williams's daughter-in-law actually gave the information to General Gillem, although one account says that she went directly to the Federal camp that afternoon and told the general exactly how to get into Greeneville by using a little-traveled street in order to avoid Morgan's pickets. Another story says that a young boy rode into Gillem's camp that night and told him that some of Morgan's men were camped on his mother's farm. One of the officers who knew the child's family was convinced he was telling the truth. As a result, the Thirteenth Tennessee, to which Private Campbell was attached, began to march and by daybreak reached Morgan's Tennessee Brigade at the fork of the Newport and Warrensburg roads, where they had been stationed the afternoon before. The pickets were asleep, so one report said, and the brigade overpowered them, opening a gap for the entry of the Federals into Greeneville. It is said that the Thirteenth Tennessee was already in Greeneville before they learned from a young Negro boy that Morgan was there "fast asleep at Miz Williams' house."

The treatment of Morgan's body after he was killed has also come in for a great deal of discussion. Some said that Private Campbell tossed it into a muddy ditch and rode away after parading it around town. However, Colonel James W. Scully, who was with General Gillem that morning after the Greeneville attack, said the general reprimanded Campbell for such disrespect for the dead, and "had the remains placed upon a caisson and carried back to Mrs. Williams' house where they were decently cared for."

In any event, the body was at Mrs. Williams's house when Captain John J. McAfee of Morgan's command returned to Greeneville under a truce flag to find out what had happened to the general. McAfee obtained a walnut casket and the general's body was placed in it.

Meanwhile, later that morning an official dispatch went out to the War Department at Washington from Bull's Gap, dated September 4, 1864: "SIR: I surprised, defeated and killed John Hunt Morgan at Greeneville, Tenn., this morning. The killed are scattered for miles, and have not yet been counted. Among the captured were Morgan's staff, with one piece of artillery and one caisson. Enemy forces outnumbered mine but the surprise was complete. Signed: General Alvin C. Gillem, U.S. Army."

11

EPILOGUE

NEWS OF MORGAN'S DEATH spread quickly throughout the nation, but many newspapers, hurrying to disseminate the word, had difficulty in getting the facts straight. Those at Lynchburg and Richmond, Virginia, reported that Morgan had been killed in battle, and it was Monday, September 5, before any word at all reached the general's widow at Abingdon.

In order to help ease the shock of the news, Mattie was first told that the general had only been injured, but even at that moment, a train bearing her husband's body was on its way from Greeneville over the same railroad on which he had ridden southward just four days earlier.

For so newsworthy an event, Abingdon's weekly newspaper, the *Virginian*, ran a comparatively modest account of the funeral. Dated Friday, September 9, it read: "BURIAL—On Monday night (Sept. 5), the remains of General Morgan arrived at Abingdon and were taken to the residence of Judge Campbell in the vicinity of where Mrs. Morgan, and one or two relatives are sojourning. On Tuesday evening at 4 o'clock, funeral services were performed by Chaplain Cameron and the procession was formed by Gen. George B. Crittenden. It was the largest and most imposing procession we have ever seen of the sort in this part of the country."

Several different units formed Crittenden's procession outside the Saint Thomas Episcopal Church where the last rites were held. As the hearse bearing the body of the slain general and unarmed bodyguards headed down the street toward the cemetery, it was followed by the chaplains from his old command; a carriage conveying the widow, Henrietta, and Basil Duke; the military family; the military court; the officers of the army; and privates and citizens. In honor of the dead Confederate cavalryman, all of the military units were mounted and marched two by two.

According to the reporter covering the event, after it was over, "the sun went down behind dark masses of clouds in the west emblematic of the sorrow and gloom that pervaded the vast concourse in attendance."

A week later the body was removed from the Abingdon cemetery and carried to Richmond, where it lay in state in the Confederate capitol. Thousands, including the general's brother Calvin, moved slowly by the modest, flag-draped coffin. "A pine box," is the way one person described it, but this makes no accounting for the walnut casket Major McAfee is said to have acquired in Greeneville shortly after Morgan was slain.

Many a Confederate great and near-great walked past the bier during the several hours the body was at the capitol; absent, however, were President Jefferson Davis and Morgan's former commanding officer, Braxton Bragg. They did not join the funeral procession, either, nor did they put in an appearance at Richmond's Hollywood Cemetery.

The Reverend George Patterson, a Confederate chaplain and friend of Morgan and Mattie, read a brief Episcopal service at the cemetery; then the body was sealed in a vault to await the end of the war, after which it would be sent to Lexington.

As everyone had hoped and expected, Basil Duke was promoted to brigadier general and placed in command of Morgan's former brigade. With a vigor he had not exhibited since before the "big raid" into Ohio, Duke and the remnants of the old command savagely attacked the Federals in the area and completely routed them from East Tennessee. Morgan would have loved the way they did it, but their victory made little or no difference as far as the final outcome of the war was concerned. In time, bigger battles fought elsewhere would seal the fate of the Confederacy, but to Duke and the Raiders—Duke's Raiders now—the victory was a very personal one.

Some of the men, including Duke, would play the drama to the bitter end. When President Davis and his cabinet, carrying the fabled Confederate treasury, fled Richmond, the escort included Duke and some of the Kentuckians—among them, several from Trigg County. When the end came, all were captured along with the president—each loyal to the last.

Three years after the war, two graves were opened—one in Virginia and the other in Kentucky. At Richmond, General John Hunt Morgan's body was removed from its sealed vault in Hollywood Cemetery; in Kentucky, the remains of the general's brother Thomas were taken from a grave in the garden of the home of the Reverend T. H. Cleland, at Lebanon. Both bodies were brought to Lexington.

A contingent of former Confederates, including General Edmund Kirby Smith, met the train bearing John Morgan's body, when it arrived from Covington the morning of April 17, 1868. A procession of men from the general's old squadron formed in front of the Phoenix Hotel and marched to Christ Church on Market Street, where the last rites were read by the rector, J. S. Shipman. Among the pallbearers were Tom Quirk, who had ridden many a mile with Morgan, and General Smith.

At the Lexington Cemetery, John Hunt Morgan and his brother were buried in the same grave, in the family plot where today most of the other members of the

Morgan family rest, including Henrietta and Basil Duke.

That April 17 was a beautiful day. White fleecy clouds floated across an otherwise brilliant blue sky. Buds were swelling in the trees; many spring blossoms were already out and the Bluegrass was fresh and green. Certainly it was a most appropriate time to come back home to Kentucky.

Bibliographical Essay

MUCH HAS BEEN WRITTEN about John Hunt Morgan since December 1861, when the nation's press carried the word that this Confederate Raider and his men had burned their first railroad trestle.

Morgan's Raiders burned many other trestles and participated in much more action before their daring leader died in 1864. Probably one of the best accounts of those exploits is *Morgan and His Raiders,* by Cecil Fletcher Holland (New York: Macmillan, 1943). Holland was most fortunate to have at his disposal a veritable treasury of Morgan's papers and letters, along with copies of his newspaper, the *Vidette,* stored and forgotten for nearly eighty years. From this material, none of which had been published before, Holland was able to put together probably the most accurate account of the real General Morgan ever written.

In 1959, Dee Alexander Brown in *The Bold Cavaliers,* (Philadelphia and New York: J. P. Lippincott), wrote of a Morgan more dashing and romantic. Both writers, as all Morgan biographers must, relied on *The Story of Morgan's Cavalry,* by Basil W. Duke. Written in 1867 when the war was still fresh in his mind, Duke put together a 578-page volume, his own eyewitness account. Although his story is somewhat biased, we can forgive Duke inasmuch as he rode alongside Morgan for most of the war. The original edition of Duke's book (Cincinnati, Ohio: Miami Printing and Publishing Co.) has been out of print for many years, but it was reprinted in 1960 by the University of Indiana Press, Bloomington, complete with an index (Duke's edition had none), editor's notes, and an introduction by Cecil Fletcher Holland.

The Civil War Centennial in 1961 rekindled interest in many Civil War personalities, including Morgan. Writers in Tennessee, Kentucky, Indiana, and Ohio in particular, did a considerable amount of research on the general's activities in those states. *Morgan's Raid in Indiana*, by Louis W. Ewbank (Fort Wayne: Indiana Historical Society, n.d.), and *The Impact of the Civil War in Indiana*, by John D. Barnhart, (Indianapolis: Indiana Civil War Centennial Commission, 1962) cover rather well Morgan's 1863 raid through Hoosierland. *The Ohio Handbook of the Civil War*, by Robert S. Harper (Columbus: Ohio Historical Society, 1961) chronicles Morgan's route as he moved from Indiana into that state.

Little known, and thus frequently overlooked by researchers, are printed accounts of the damage Morgan did to the L & N Railroad in Kentucky and Tennessee during the war. Albert Fink, an L & N official whose duty it was to repair the war damage, wrote lengthy reports of his rebuilding, which often began before the ashes of the burned bridges had cooled. His accounts were published in the railroad's annual report to stockholders during each of the war years. These annual reports have long been out of print, but they later were excerpted by Joseph G. Kerr and published in his *Historical Development of the Louisville & Nashville Railroad System*. This book was privately printed by the L & N in 1926, but copies are still available in some libraries. A reading of Fink's accounts along with Duke's story provides the reader with a rare eyewitness account of activities on both sides. Duke was hired by the L & N's law department after the war, and one of his first chores was to meet Fink and compare notes.

Historical society quarterlies and popular magazines have published and continue to publish numerous articles about Morgan and the Raiders. In most cases such essays cover specific segments of Morgan's military operations. The most popular of these has been his second raid into Kentucky, more often called the Christmas Raid. The most recent account is a four-part series by Edwin C. Bearss, "Morgan's Second Kentucky Raid, December 1862" (*Kentucky Historical Society Register* 70–72 [July 1972, April 1973, October 1973, January 1974]). Other good accounts of that same raid include Hal Engerud's "Morgan's Christmas Raid" (*L & N Magazine*, December 1932) and Charles B. Castner's "General Morgan's Christmas Party in Kentucky" (*L & N Magazine*, December 1962). Probably Mr. Bearss, who is with the National Park Service Office of History, has written the most detailed account, largely because of his reliance on and ready access to official records. The Filson Club, Louisville, of which Albert Fink was a lifetime member, has published a long list of articles about Morgan in its *Quarterly*. Of special interest is "John Hunt Morgan and the Soldier Printers," by Howard D. Doll (January 1973); "A Federal Officer Pursues John Hunt Morgan," by Lowell H. Harrison, (April 1974), and "The Death of John Hunt Morgan," by Harry Harris (January 1965). Many fine stories have appeared also in the *Civil War Times Illustrated*, among them "A Thunderbolt out of the South," by Stephen E. Ambrose (June 1963).

In 1961–1965, during the Centennial of the Civil War, newspapers in many parts of the country published numerous specialized and well-illustrated articles. One of the best of these was the Sunday supplement "The Civil War in Kentucky, Centennial 1861–1865," edited by the late Joe Creason (Louisville *Courier-Journal*, November 2, 1960). Another very comprehensive supplement was "The Civil War in Middle Tennessee," by Ed Huddleston. Originally published by the Nashville *Banner* in four separate issues, one during each year of the Centennial, it later was assembled in book form (Parthenon Press, 1965). Although Huddleston's account covers all wartime activities in Tennessee, he devoted a generous amount of space to Morgan and his Raiders.

Newspaper files of the Civil War period also provide a wealth of Morgan material. A surprising number of papers published during the war are extant and have been preserved on microfilm by various historical organizations and state and public libraries. The *Louisville Journal*, which during the war carried George Prentice's frequent and often biting editorial comment, contains much data. This paper and others published in Louisville during that time are available on microfilm at the Free Public Library and the Filson Club. In Tennessee, the *Nashville Daily Union*, the *Murfreesboro Daily Rebel Banner* and the *Lebanon Herald*, among many others, are on film at the Tennessee State Library and Archives at Nashville.

Researchers today feel that all the important material pertaining to Morgan has been found. Nothing new has turned up since Cecil Holland made the so-called Williamson papers public in 1943. These papers had been preserved by Mattie Morgan, who, after the general's death, married Judge W. H. Williamson of Lebanon, Tennessee. Most of them are now in the Southern Historical Collection of the University of North Carolina, Chapel Hill. Various other universities, including the University of Kentucky, also have Morgan collections.